4|5|06

Faith Studie
Ethics
For AQA

ASSESSMENT and
QUALIFICATIONS
ALLIANCE

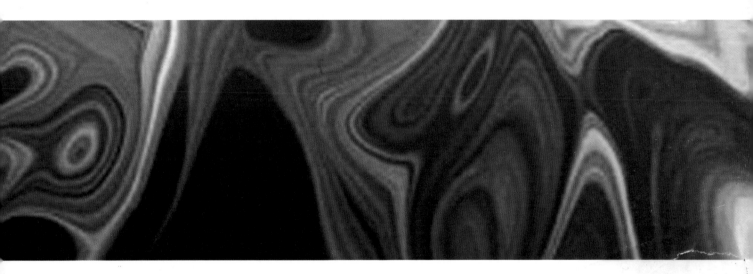

Lesley Parry

Hodder Murray
A MEMBER OF THE HODDER HEADLINE GROUP

Many thanks go to JRH and Viv for their patience, cups of tea, time and help. Thanks to Irfanah for her help. Thanks to Nadezda for the faith she shows in my ability to write these books! I dedicate it to all those who have struggled and taught this course without a specific textbook – now you've got one! And also to all those studying the course – let me know what I need to change for next time because this book is for you and your success.

The Publishers would like to thank the following for permission to reproduce copyright material:

Credits
All illustrations by Barking Dog Art.
Photos:
Alamy: Westend61/Alamy: page 50 (*left*), Janine Wiedel Photolibrary/Alamy: page 52 (*top left*), ImageState/Alamy: page 54 (*bottom right*), Israel Images/Alamy: page 75 (*bottom*), page 80, Stock Connection/Alamy: page 88 (*2nd from top*), David Levenson/Alamy: page 89 (*bottom left*), AGStock USA, Inc/Alamy: page 91 (*left*), Jack Sullivan/Alamy: page 91 (*middle*), The Anthony Blake Photo Library/Alamy: page 93 (*2nd from top*). CIRCA Photo Library/William Holtby: pages 2 and 3 (*middle*), page 4 (*bottom*), CIRCA Photo Library/John Smith: page 9 (*top*), CIRCA Photo Library/Bipin J. Mistry: page 12 and 13 (*middle*). Corbis: Corbis/Luc Hosten; Gallo Images: page 1 (*bottom right*), Corbis/James Marshall: page 4 (*2nd from top*), Corbis/Alison Wright: page 4 (*2nd from bottom*), Corbis/Chris Lisle: page 5 (*top*), Corbis/David Samuel Robbins: page 6 (*top*), Corbis/Richard Powers: page 6 (*bottom*), Corbis/Dave Bartruff: page 9 (*2nd from top*), Corbis/Michael Nicholson: page 12 (*top left*), Desmond Boylan/Reuters/Corbis: page 14 (*top*), Corbis/Gary Braasch: page 14 (*2nd from top*), Sherwin Crasto/Reuters/Corbis: page 14 (*2nd from bottom*), Corbis/Ashley Cooper: page 21 (*2nd from top*), Corbis/Ted Spiegel: page 22 (*middle left*), page 24 (*bottom*), Corbis/David H. Wells: page 24 (*top*), page 25, Corbis/Richard T. Nowitz: page 26 (*top left*), Corbis/Randy Faris: page 57, Corbis/Owen Franken: page 69 (*bottom left*), Corbis/Paul Almasy: page 71, Corbis/Steve Raymer: page 72 (*top*), Corbis/Richard T. Nowitz: page 75 (*top*), Bazuki Muhammad/Reuters/Corbis: page 81. Lesley Parry: page 1 (*top left, top middle, top right, bottom left, bottom middle*), page 2 (*top left, bottom left*), page 3 (*top right, bottom right*), page 5 (*bottom*), page 6 (*top right*), page 7 (*top right*), page 8 (*top left*), page 9 (*2nd from top, bottom*), page 10 (*2nd from top, bottom*), page 11 (*right*), page 12 (*bottom*), page 14 (*left*), page 17 (*bottom*), page 18 (*left top and bottom*), page 19, page 20, page 21 (*left, right: top, 2nd from bottom and bottom*), page 22 (*top left, bottom left*), page 26 (*top right*), page 28 (*top left*), page 72 (*bottom*), page 77, page 79, page 88 (*bottom*), page 93 (*top, 2nd from bottom*), page 97, page 106. E & E Picture Library: page 8 and 9 (*middle*). Empics: Malcolm Browne/Empics: page 39, Abaca Press/Empics: page 55 (*top*), Tina Fineberg/Empics: page 55 (*bottom*). FARE: page 51. Hutchison Pictures/Eye Ubiquitous: page 24 (*2nd from bottom*). Ingram: page 93 (*middle, bottom*). Israelimages/Rex Features page 26 (*bottom left*). Photodisc: page 50 (*top right and bottom right*), page 53, page 54 (*top left*), page 60, page 62, page 89 (*top left, bottom right*). Photofusion: Paula Solloway/Photofusion: page 10 (*top*), Colin Edwards/Photofusion: page 11 (*left*), Judy Harrison/Photofusion: page 12 (left middle), page 14 (*bottom*), page 27 (*bottom right*), page 31 (*2nd from top, left*), page 76 (*bottom*), page 22 and 23 (*middle*), Paul Doyle/Photofusion: page 29 (*bottom*), page 31 (*bottom*), page 59, page 69 (*top right*), Photofusion Picture Library/Alamy: page 51 (*top right*), Maggie Murray/Photofusion: page 52 (*middle*), Peter Olive/Photofusion: page 52 (*bottom left*), Gina Glover/Photofusion: page 68, Steve Morgan/Photofusion: page 89 (*top right*), Jo Lawbuary/Photofusion: page 90 (*top*), A Sanger Davis/Photofusion: page 90 (*middle*), Joanne O'Brien/Photofusion: page 90 (*bottom*), Steve Morgan/Photofusion: page 91 (*right*). RSPCA Photo Library: page 88 (*top*). Sonia Halliday Photographs: page 18 and 19 (*middle*). World Religions Photo Library – Christine Osborne: page 4 (*top*), page 7 (*top left, bottom right*), page 10 (*2nd from bottom*), page 15, page 16, page 17 (*top*), page 23 (*right*), page 24 (*2nd from top*), page 27 (*top left*), page 28 (*bottom left*), page 28 and 29 (*middle*), page 29 (*top*), page 30, page 31 (*top, 2nd from bottom*), page 70, page 74, page 76 (*top*), page 78.

Acknowledgements
The Qur'an: Basic Teachings, Irving/Ahmad/Ahsan, Islamic Foundation, 1979.
AQA Specification B & C Anthology of Religious Texts, 2002.
Holy Bible: New International Version, Hodder and Stoughton, 1973.

Every effort has been made to trace all copyright holders, but if any have been inadvertently overlooked the Publishers will be pleased to make the necessary arrangements at the first opportunity.

Although every effort has been made to ensure that website addresses are correct at time of going to press, Hodder Murray cannot be held responsible for the content of any website mentioned in this book. It is sometimes possible to find a relocated web page by typing in the address of the home page for a website in the URL window of your browser.

Orders: please contact Bookpoint Ltd, 130 Milton Park, Abingdon, Oxon OX14 4SB. Telephone: (44) 01235 827720. Fax: (44) 01235 400454. Lines are open 9.00 – 6.00, Monday to Saturday, with a 24-hour message answering service. Visit our website at www.hoddereducation.co.uk

> Words printed in SMALL CAPITALS (first mention only)
> are defined in the Glossary on pages 111–113.

© Lesley Parry 2006
First published in 2006 by
Hodder Murray, an imprint of Hodder Education,
a member of the Hodder Headline Group
338 Euston Road
London NW1 3BH

Impression number	10 9 8 7 6 5 4 3 2 1
Year	2010 2009 2008 2007 2006

Cover photo: Digital Vision/Getty Images.
Typeset in 10.5/12 pt Stone Serif by DC Graphic Design Ltd, Swanley, Kent
Printed in Italy

A catalogue record for this title is available from the British Library.

ISBN-10: 0 340 90656 1
ISBN-13: 978 0 340 90656 9

Contents

....

Introduction

This book is designed to provide a basis of knowledge to help any student in the pursuit of a GCSE short course award for the AQA Specification B course, Faith Studies and Ethics.

The book covers all aspects of the specification in each of the six religions. It tries to show links between the elements of the specification, so that students are better prepared for seeing questions that mix the different topics. Students have to study two world religions for this course, and have to answer all questions from the point of view of the same two religions throughout their examination paper. This book goes far beyond what any one class needs and gives teachers the flexibility to tailor the choice of religions to each class or even student if they want to. Teachers will always be able to supplement the book with additional ideas and arguments, but the book provides more than is necessary for the exam in the first place.

Written by a Senior Examiner for AQA, the text gives guidance on the styles of questions that can be asked and the depth of knowledge that better candidates are expected to show. Questions always have to be answerable from all six perspectives, and this shapes both the range and style of questions available to be set.

The themes for the course are:

Theme A: Worship

a) Public and private worship

b) Places of worship

Theme B: Relationships, Rights and Responsibilities

Evaluative questions

There are many examples of evaluative questions, which provide one quarter of the total marks on the examination paper. Candidates need to have a good technique, and this is addressed. The most common problems candidates have is in responding to the exact quotation rather than arguing about a topic, so they would benefit from working as a class to unroll the whole range of potential responses until they are confident enough to tackle them on their own.

The issues

Up to a third of the marks on the paper are for explaining how religions respond to different issues. It is important for candidates to use beliefs and teachings in their answers as they explain attitudes to the issues. The beliefs and teachings are highlighted in each section.

Visual images

The book includes many images, especially in the section on worship, to help any student get a visual idea of what they are studying. However, encourage students to collect a range of their own images, which will help them to explore similarities between and within the religions. This will reinforce the elements they may need to know for the examination. It also gives them a visual reference to call to mind in exams, which – for some – is best suited to their learning style.

Research tasks

Research tasks are included to extend student knowledge and thinking on some matters. These do not form necessary knowledge for the examination, but provide extension work for gifted students. All students could also be encouraged to supplement their ethics work with newspaper articles. This helps them to appreciate the range of moral views on any topic, and is a vital part of being able to address the evaluative questions at the top grade levels. It will also help them to understand the issues themselves, if they see them described in a variety of ways. They also provide up-to-date examples to use in answers.

The specification refers to studies of organisations – local, national and international. The examination can ask about the work of an organisation in any of the focus topics, so students will find it helpful to do some research about linked organisations for each topic. Some are suggested in the book.

Revision and exam tips

Throughout the text, there are revision and exam tips. It should prove valuable to check them all out – not just those that sit in the religions you are studying – because they are all different. They have been placed as a feature for easy spotting.

Encourage your students to keep a glossary of terms for all their technical language, and encourage them also to keep a notebook of exam tips. As they come across new types of both exam tips and phrases, they can jot them down for themselves. One small notebook suffices for both, used from one end as a glossary, and from the other as an exam revision tip book.

1 Worship

Recognising places of worship from the outside

Religious buildings are often very distinctive from the outside. Even if the building has no obvious religious markings, it is still easy to recognise as a place of WORSHIP.

How can you tell if a building is a place of worship?

It might just look religious, or you might be able to tell to which religion it belongs. Most religious buildings have a sign giving their name and telling you about service times and so on, making them fairly easy to recognise. There might be people who are obviously going there to worship – carrying a BIBLE, for example, or wearing PRAYER clothes. The buildings may also have some symbols of their faith, such as the crescent moon on a MOSQUE or the Star of David over a SYNAGOGUE door.

Many religious buildings can be recognised by their distinctive style – for instance, many have a tower, such as CHURCHES, mosques (where it is called a minaret) and Hindu TEMPLES. The decoration might also make it obvious – for example, mosques often have geometrical patterns, and Hindu temples have carvings of gods.

Research Task —

Look at the photos below, can you work out which building belongs to which religion?

Buddhists worship at temples.

Christians worship at churches.

Hindus worship at mandirs (temples).

Muslims worship at mosques.

Jews worship at synagogues.

Sikhs worship at gurdwaras.

The Basics

①
For each of the two religions you are studying, name their place of worship.

②
Use the pictures from this page – for each of the two religions you are studying, write down what makes it obvious that the building is a religious building.

③
Collect three images of different religious buildings for the two religions you are studying. On each, label the features that help us to see to which religion it belongs.

Looking inside a Buddhist temple

The photos above and on the right are the outside and inside of different Buddhist temples.

The **SHRINE** is the name given to the front display in the temple where the statue of the Buddha is located. Worshippers come to the SHRINE to show their devotion and to place offerings. The shrine often has many other statues of the BUDDHA around it.

Many Buddhists bow down on the floor **(PROSTRATE)** in front of the shrine. This shows respect for the teachings of the Buddha.

The **STATUE OF THE BUDDHA** usually shows him sitting in a MEDITATION pose. He wears monk's robes and his long hair is a reminder that he was a prince. His hands have a symbolic set position, called a mudra. This image shows the mudra of bearing witness. It refers to when Gotama (Buddha) called to the earth to prove that he deserved to become enlightened – to see the true nature of all things, and so be released from the cycle of rebirth. He sits on a lotus flower, the symbol for enlightenment.

The Basics

① Explain what each of the following items, often found in Buddhist temples, are: shrine, statues, offerings.

② Draw a labelled diagram of the inside of a temple. Make sure you include notes about each item within it.

③ Find pictures of each of the items for your own notes. Research their importance and use.

④ 'Shrines can be made anywhere and still be as important.' Do you agree with this statement? Write three reasons why you agree and three reasons why you disagree. For each reason, try to explain yourself, either by giving examples or by writing more fully.

Buddhists buy bunches of **INCENSE** sticks, which they light and place in a container before they go into the shrine room. The incense reminds them that the teachings of the Buddha are sweet and everlasting.

STATUES of the Buddha are found on the shrine. The largest of the statues sits in the centre. Different temples have varying numbers of statues. Extra statues may show the Buddha seated, standing up or lying down. They will be made from various materials such as gold, wood or stone. The style is usually a reflection of the country and its culture – in Western temples, the Buddha may have European features.

OFFERINGS are made as an act of worship.

1. The **FLOWERS** remind us of anicca (impermanence), meaning everything changes. Although the flowers are beautiful, they will die. In Asian countries, the flowers offered are usually lotus flowers.

2. As well as being burnt outside the shrine room, **INCENSE STICKS** may be lit and put in small numbers as OFFERINGS on the actual shrine.

3. **CANDLES** or lamps are found in shrine rooms. They symbolise the light of the Buddha's teachings, helping us to see the right way to live and become free from rebirth.

4. Worshippers leave **FOOD AND MONEY** offerings to show their gratitude for the Buddha's teachings. Monks, who live at and run the temple, eat the food and the money helps with the upkeep of the temple.

Worship in Buddhism

Worshipping at home

Many Buddhists have shrines at home where they make a daily act of worship. Home shrines include one or more statues of the Buddha, candles and incense. Worshippers will light some incense and bow to the statue, as they chant prayers and mantras. Buddhists often meditate in front of the shrine. Meditation is one part of the Noble Eightfold Path, the eight areas of self-discipline that Buddhists practise to try to achieve enlightenment.

Worshipping in a temple

Buddhist temples are often very colourful places, with many statues of the Buddha. Worshippers will bring flowers, incense and food offerings to the temple as an act of worship. They may buy them at special stalls. The worshippers prepare themselves by burning incense outside the shrine room. Then they will take off their shoes before entering the shrine room and walking to the front of the room. They place the flowers and other offerings on the shrine as a gift, and step back with their hands together to bow before the statue. This is a sign of their devotion to the teachings of the Buddha. At this point, worshippers can ask for something in prayer. Many will chant prayers or mantras. They may kneel and meditate in the shrine room, or outside it, or may seek advice or teaching from one of the monks. The most common form of worship is as an individual at the temple.

Buddhists may also worship as a group. On special days, they arrive at the temple, remove their shoes, make their offerings and prostrate. Then they take places in the shrine room, where they begin to meditate quietly. After a period of time, the leader of the temple will give a short sermon or teaching to the group to help their understanding of Buddhism.

Use these pictures to remember the details of Buddhist worship. Describe what you see and you will have a good idea of the main elements of an act of worship.

Buddhists remove their shoes before going into the shrine room.

Buddhists make offerings to the Buddha.

They will prostrate before before a statue of the Buddha.

They may listen to a sermon led by a monk.

Meditation

All Buddhists learn to meditate. This is the act of focusing on something specific, for example, an idea or an image. Meditation stills and calms the mind – the same as when the surface of a pool of water is calm, we can see the bottom clearly. This allows the meditator to see and understand religious truths. It takes a lot of practice and self-discipline to be able to meditate for long periods of time.

There are many types of meditation:

- Samatha meditation concerns 'one-pointedness of mind' – focusing on one thing to calm the mind and see clearly. This kind of meditation allows the person to get control of their mind, so that they can begin to analyse spiritual truths.

- Metta bhavana is a form of Samatha meditation that concentrates on love and compassion. This helps to get rid of negative and destructive thoughts.

- Vipassana meditation aims to achieve an insight into the true nature of things – to discover that the world is emptiness and nothingness. The Samatha method builds up to this kind of meditation.

So why do Buddhists meditate?

One reason is to follow the Buddha's example in order to achieve enlightenment. He also taught that meditation was important – it is part of the Noble Eightfold Path. It is a form of self-development, which is one of the main aims of Buddhism. It allows the worshipper to have an insight into the true nature of things, and Buddhism seeks that goal. Meditation also aids health and well-being.

A Buddhist monk meditating. Meditation is a big part of daily life for monks.

Aids to worship

Buddhists use many things to help their focus in worship and meditation. Any statue or image of the Buddha displays a lot of symbols that help the worshipper to think of the Buddha's life or teachings, or both. Monks also create mandalas – complex coloured patterns made out of different colours of sand that are formed and then left to be blown away or swept up. Buddhists often use a set of prayer beads too, called MALA, as a focus for chanting. Buddhists also use prayer wheels containing written prayers. When the worshipper spins the wheel, the prayers are sent. The sights and smells of the temple all help in the act of worship, as they are reminders of the Buddha's teachings (see pages 2–3).

Buddhist prayer beads and a prayer wheel.

Research Task –

Find a picture of a mandala. Find out how they are made and what they symbolise.

Buddhist religious leaders

In Buddhism, followers look to the leaders known as BHIKKHUS (in Theravada Buddhism) for guidance on how to live their lives as Buddhists. Monks and nuns are treated with the greatest respect (see above). They focus on following the Buddha's teachings, and on gaining enlightenment. They are following a path set out by the Buddha himself at the start of the religion, and they do not allow the world to distract them. Buddhism does not have religious ceremonies for marriage, death, etc., but monks will perform blessings for the lay community. Buddhists can carry out their own personal ceremonies but monks do not always attend as their role means that they renounce all worldly things, including parties or ceremonies. Local communities support the monks financially. Most Buddhists make offerings to the shrines at their temple, knowing that the food and money will be used to support the monks.

A symbol of Buddhism

This is the DHARMACHAKRA. *Dharma* is the name for guidance to the Buddhist way of living. The eight spokes represent the eight stages of the Noble Eightfold Path. As a circle or wheel, it can be seen to represent the cycle of rebirth – birth, death and rebirth.

Buddhist sacred writings

There are many different sacred writings in Buddhism, reflecting the many strands of the religion and the many cultures that follow the faith. Together the writings (see above) are known as the TIPITAKA, or three baskets, because there are three groups of texts. The first focuses on the rules of behaviour for monks in all areas of their lives; the second on what the Buddha and his disciples taught; and the third group describes Buddhist philosophy. They help Buddhists to understand their religion and to know how to live within its teachings.

Buddhists might meditate on the teachings found in the scriptures. They could attend a lecture by a monk about the teachings, or they may have their own copies of some texts that they read and try to understand. In both cases, their goal is to strengthen their understanding of the Buddha's teaching.

Revision tip

When you are trying to remember how to describe something, list the key terms. This list will act like a set of coat hangers for the rest of your knowledge. If you can only remember the list, you will still get about half the available marks. For example, the main features of a Buddhist act of worship are incense, shoes, offerings and prostration.

Answer the questions on page 32 about Buddhist worship.

Christian religious leaders

There are many different types of religious leaders. Most branches of Christianity have their own named person, for example, VICAR, priest (see above), pastor and minister. Essentially, they all carry out the same role – they lead services, perform ceremonies and look after the pastoral care of their congregation. Many have had formal training, either a university degree or training at a religious college. They are usually appointed by a higher body to a position within the Church, and may be moved to a different church after a period of time. Some Christian groups, such as Anglicans, have a hierarchy of posts, so ministers progress in their careers as religious leaders.

Revision tip

Lots of religions share the same reasons for why things are important. Learn the general reason and add a specific example for each of your two religions. For example, Question – why are religious leaders important? Answer – they have studied hard so they know the teachings well. Christian religious leaders have usually spent many years studying at a university or seminary.

Symbols of Christianity

There are two major symbols of Christianity – the CROSS and the CRUCIFIX. Christianity is based around the teachings of Jesus Christ. These symbols remind Christians of him. The crucifix is a reminder that Jesus was crucified and died as a sacrifice for mankind's sins. The cross symbolises that Jesus rose again from the dead to eternal life. This is what Christians hope – that they will be raised from death to be with God in heaven.

Christian sacred writings

The Bible, (see above) made up of the Old and New Testaments, is the Christian holy book. The story and teachings of Jesus and the early Christians are found in the New Testament. These guide the follower on how God wants them to live their lives, so that they can ultimately get to heaven. The Bible helps Christians to understand more about God and their faith. Some believe it is the actual word of God, while others believe that it is inspired by God.

Answer the questions on page 32 about Christian worship.

Looking inside a Christian church

The photos on the left and on the right are the outside and inside of different churches.

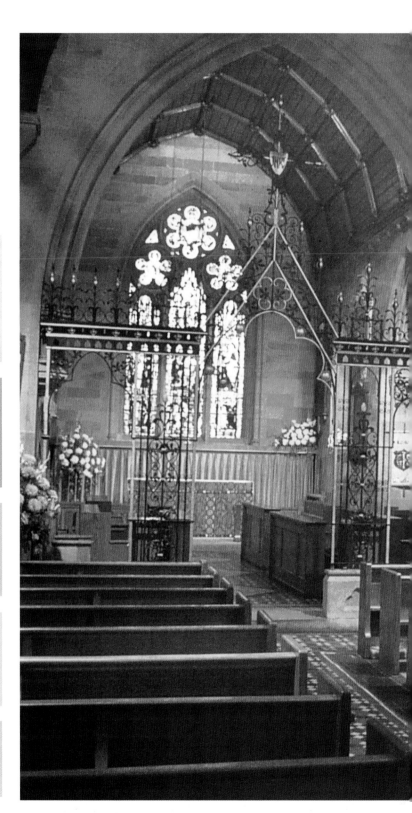

The **CROSS** is the symbol of Christianity. Jesus was executed on a cross on Good Friday and rose from the dead on Easter Sunday. These events are the focus of the Christian faith. A cross with a figure of Jesus on it is called a **CRUCIFIX**. This reminds Christians of Jesus' sacrifice.

The **ALTAR** is the focal point of the church. It represents the holiest part of the church and is often behind a barrier like a COMMUNION rail. The bread and wine are kept on the ALTAR, which represents the table from the Last Supper.

The **COMMUNION RAIL** is where the church members kneel to take communion. It is often as close to the altar as anyone other than the priest will get. It could be a line or a physical barrier.

BREAD AND COMMUNION WINE are used for Holy Communion, to remember the sacrifice of Jesus for all mankind. The bread represents the body of Christ and the wine represents his blood.

STAINED GLASS WINDOWS are coloured windows, often with religious pictures from the life of Jesus or one of the saints. They inform and inspire the worshippers.

Readings from the Bible are made from the **LECTERN**. Many have a carving of an eagle on them. This represents St John and the inspiration of the Gospels. The **PULPIT** is where the minister stands to preach a sermon. It is a raised platform, and this high position shows the importance of delivering God's message. From the pulpit, the minister is visible to everyone when he or she preaches so they can hear and see him or her speak the word of God.

The congregation sit in **PEWS** – long benches that imply that everyone is the same and equal before God. Modern churches are more likely to have rows of individual chairs. Music is an important part of a church service and many churches have an **ORGAN** or a music group. Both are used throughout the service, but especially to accompany hymn-singing. Church music is inspired by religious belief, and therefore encourages those singing or listening to think of God.

Babies are baptised at the **FONT**. In old churches, it is near the door as a welcoming sign. In more modern churches, it is more central and often near the front. This implies that the congregation will look after the child's spiritual welfare. In Baptist churches, there is a baptistery where adults can be baptised by total immersion.

The Basics

① Explain what each of the following items, often found in churches, are: altar, cross, pulpit, lectern, font, communion rail, pews.

② Draw a labelled diagram of the inside of a church. Make sure you include notes about each item within it.

③ Find pictures of each of the items for your own notes. Research their importance and use.

④ 'It is okay to worship God anywhere – you don't need a holy building.' Do you agree with this statement? Write three reasons why you agree and three reasons why you disagree. For each reason, try to explain yourself, either by giving examples or by writing more fully.

Worship in Christianity

The congregation stands to sing hymns.

Worship in a church

Christians usually go to church to worship. This may be to reflect alone or to be part of a congregation. The main holy day is Sunday, when most services are held. Sunday remembers the day of rest after God had created the world. It also keeps the commandment to keep one day holy and reminds Christians that Jesus rose from the dead on a Sunday.

The congregation bow their heads in prayer.

When Catholic and Orthodox Christians enter a church, they usually make the sign of the cross and genuflect (a kind of bow) to show their respect. Church services usually begin with a hymn. In Anglican churches, the vicar often comes in during this hymn and the Bible is brought into the church with him. A prayer usually follows the first hymn, and then another hymn. There will be one or more readings from the Bible – often one from the Old and one from the New Testament – followed by a sermon that will be linked to the readings, the day or recent events. The sermon teaches about the faith and its practice. Services usually end with a hymn, followed by the prayer of benediction. During a service, a collection will be made – some Christians give up to ten per cent of their wages as a gift to the church. In some denominations the services are less formal and the form of the service varies each week. Worship, it is claimed, is led by the Holy Spirit and in charismatic or Pentecostal churches, members may speak in tongues (verbal sounds produced by religious ecstasy) or give prophecies. In Quaker meetings there are often long periods of silence before a worshipper feels prompted to speak.

Readings are made from the Bible – one from each of the Old and New Testaments.

The Communion service (also called Eucharist, the Lord's Supper or Mass) is an important part of worship. It commemorates the Last Supper, when Jesus broke bread and gave wine to his disciples. These represented his body and blood, and therefore the sacrifice he was about to make for humankind. Christians today (except Quakers and members of the Salvation Army) follow the service in remembrance of Jesus, of his sacrifice and as a symbol of a fresh start after being forgiven. Traditions like this date back to Jesus' time and are performed by most Christians.

Christians give money as an offering.

Use these pictures to remember the details of Christian worship. Describe what you see and you will have a good idea of the main elements of a service.

Prayer

A small girl prays in the pews of a church.

Prayer is a way of speaking to God. Jesus taught and gave his disciples a special prayer to say called the Lord's Prayer. This prayer takes all the things we do in prayer – asking for things, seeking forgiveness, saying thank you – and adds praise of God, to create what Christians consider to be the perfect prayer. Most Christians also pray without using set prayers, and say what is most relevant to their lives at that time. They might also study the Bible and their prayers help them to understand what they have read. This is similar to meditation in that they are trying to work out a spiritual truth.

So why do Christians pray?

Praying is a tradition within Christianity. Christians are taught to pray and to make it part of their normal religious practice. This practice gives Christians a sense of community and solidarity. Originally, Jesus taught his disciples how to pray, and so this ritual has a connection to Jesus. It is a way to contact God and many Christians feel that they have experienced God through prayer. Christian mystics pray for long periods of time, hoping to understand clearly spiritual truths and to experience God. Their whole lives are based around achieving both of these things through prayer and meditation. Lots of Christians say that prayer makes them feel better – the idea that someone is listening makes them feel special and can help to solve problems.

Aids to worship

You have already learned about the cross and crucifix, symbols that most Christians carry. They act as a focus and reminder of the most important parts of the faith – that Jesus gave his life as a sacrifice for mankind and that he rose from the dead. Many Christians, especially in the Catholic and Orthodox traditions, have prayer beads. These are called rosary beads in the Roman Catholic faith. They help the worshipper to focus on a prayer that they repeat, or to meditate on events in Jesus' life.

Christians use icons and rosary beads as aids to worship.

Pictures or icons of Jesus, Mary and the saints are often seen in the homes of Christians, especially Catholic and Orthodox believers. These are reminders of their importance in the faith, but can also act as a focus for meditation and prayer.

Research Task —

Find out more about rosary beads — what they look like, what they symbolise and how they are used.

Looking inside a Hindu mandir

The photos above and on the right are the outside and inside of different Hindu MANDIRS.

The **MAIN SHRINE** is called the garba griha. It is usually central in the furthest wall from the door. It is the biggest shrine, and it is where the BRAHMIN PRIESTS focus most of their work. The shrine centres around the deity to whom the temple is dedicated. It has a main statue for the deity; offerings, such as flowers and food; and other symbols of Hinduism, such as the aum sign. The deity often has garlands of flowers draped over it, which are gifts from the worshippers.

SIDE SHRINES are found along the side walls of the temple and are usually smaller and less imposing than the main shrine. Again, there is a statue or picture of the deity, as well as offerings from the worshippers.

A **BELL** is found at each shrine. When the worshippers begin to pray, one of them rings a bell to awaken the presence of the deity within the shrine.

HINDU SYMBOLS are usually found on the different shrines. The most common symbols are the swastika, which is supposed to bring good fortune, and the AUM symbol, which is the symbol for Hinduism. Aum is thought of as the sound of the universe being created and is used as a mantra, to be repeated during worship.

An **ARTI TRAY** is for one specific type of worship, which takes place many times each day. It consists of a tray with a lamp on it, lit by five wicks, which worshippers pass their hands through and then touch their forehead, as a kind of blessing.

HOLY WATER is called charanamrita, and is the water left after bathing the statues of the deities. As a kind of blessing, the worshippers sprinkle some of this onto themselves after praying.

Each temple has its own **BRAHMIN PRIEST** or a team of them. Their job is based in the temple, but includes a lot of teaching work for the younger people in the community and giving scriptural advice to the worshippers.

The Basics

Explain what each of the following items, often found in mandirs, are: garba griha, Hindu symbols, side shrines, bell, charanamrita.

Draw a labelled diagram of the inside of a mandir. Make sure you include notes about each item within it.

Find pictures of each of the items for your own notes. Research their importance and use.

'We can really understand God through the statues that represent him.' Do you agree with this statement? Write three reasons why you agree and three reasons why you disagree. For each reason, try to explain yourself, either by giving examples or by writing more fully.

Worship in Hinduism

Like everything else in Hinduism, worship takes many forms. The exam will only ask and credit you for a basic description of a Hindu act of worship, so you have lots to choose from in your revision.

The arti ceremony.

Puja

Hindus have their own shrines at home (see left) and will carry out a PUJA every morning there. This is worship of a particular deity. The exact form of the puja differs from family to family, but there are some general things that happen. The statue of the deity is washed and dressed. Gifts of water and flowers are made, and an offering of food is given. Throughout the ritual, the worshipper chants prayers or a mantra.

Hindus making offerings to a deity.

Arti

At the end of the puja, Hindus carry out the arti ceremony. This is a ceremony to greet the deity – the worshipper offers different items to the deity by moving them in a circular motion in front of it. These include incense, flowers, water and lamps. At the same time, they ring a bell and meditate on the deity. The worshippers draw their hands over the lighted flame and touch their foreheads. They take back some of the flowers and sprinkle water on themselves. In the temple, the priest carries out the same ritual. Afterwards there is kirtan and bhajan, the singing of hymns.

Havan – the fire sacrifice.

Darshan

Many Hindus make an act of devotion to one particular deity. This is called darshan, which means seeing. The worshipper stands before the deity (or holy person) and bows their head, holding their hands together. Some prostrate to show their respect. They give a gift of flowers, food and/or money, and say some prayers. Then they drink a little holy water (charanamrita) and are given some of the sacred food (prashad). This is the most common form of worship seen in temples, when the arti or puja ceremonies have not been held.

There are other forms of worship you could see if you went to a temple. At weddings and festivals, you might see havan, the fire sacrifice. While chanting, worshippers offer grains of rice and ghee butter to the flame of a lamp.

Religious leaders give sermons to groups. These are based on Hindu teachings and worshippers are allowed to ask questions afterwards to improve their understanding. This is called pravachan, which is a separate act of worship. Many Hindus also buy study books in order to learn the scriptures and teachings in their own time.

Hindus singing hymns together in the temple.

Use these pictures to remember the details of Hindu worship. Describe what you see and you will have a good idea of the main elements of a service.

Meditation and prayer

Prayers and meditation are both very important in Hinduism. Most forms of worship need prayers as part of the ceremony. Meditation on religious teachings is encouraged as Hindus seek to purify their soul (atman) to attain a better REINCARNATION.

So why do Hindus pray?

Many Hindus believe that, by prayer and meditation, they are less likely to behave badly. This is because thay are concentrating on religious truths. This increases their chances of a better reincarnation because their soul is purer. Prayer or meditation can be a way to experience the Ultimate Reality. For many, it is simply a tradition and is a natural part of their religion.

Aids to worship

Think of all of the elements of the shrine that help the worshipper to focus – images, symbols, incense, the bell and so on. All these things are an attempt to help the worshipper to concentrate and remember the teachings of the religion. Many Hindus use a set of 108 beads, called a mala, to help them when chanting or meditating. Some Hindus find that chanting mantras aids their concentration. Often the mantra calls to one of the deities.

Coloured patterns called rangoli may be drawn while chanting or praying in temple courtyards. Often these are done for rituals and festivals. Many Hindus practise yoga, which is a physical discipline that needs concentration and effort. It is common to meditate while doing yoga. Yoga is one of the Hindu systems for achieving nirvana – freedom from the cycle of reincarnation.

> **Research Task —**
>
> Find out more details about one of these acts of worship — darshan, havan or arti. Find out about rangoli patterns.

Some Hindus practise yoga to help achieve nirvana.

Hindu religious leaders

All Hindu temples have one or more priests (see left). Usually they are from the Brahmin section of the community, and are almost always men (except in ISKCON, the Krishna Consciousness movement). They lead all of the services at the temple, both regular and special ceremonies. They are trained in their role and have a good understanding of the scriptures. Those who are especially knowledgeable because of their studies are called pandits. All must follow certain sets of rules, for example, dietary rules and rules against alcohol or drugs. Many worshippers will go to them for advice. The priests are also able to write and read horoscopes, which are important in Hinduism.

Hindu sacred writings

There are many sacred texts in Hinduism and these can be split into two groups – shruti and smriti. The shruti (those which are heard) are the most important and include what are thought to be eternal truths from the Ultimate Reality. The famous Veda scriptures are part of the shruti texts. The smriti (those which are remembered) are additional texts, including epic stories, such as the Mahabharata. The teachings in the shruti form the foundations of Hinduism, but the smriti help the worshipper to understand more fully. The scriptures are read at festivals, during pravachan in the temple and as part of personal study (see above). All sacred texts are treated with great respect. For example, they are never placed directly on the floor and worshippers wash before reading them.

A symbol of Hinduism

The most famous symbol of Hinduism is the aum symbol. Aum is the sound chanted by many Hindus when offering worship. It is said to be the sound of the universe and the sound made when the universe was created. Just saying this sound is a holy act for Hindus. The symbol is seen at every shrine, home or temple.

Revision tip

Learn the 'What – How – Why' formula for everything – *What* is it? *How* is it used? *Why* is it important? These are the three most common types of exam questions. For example, *What* is a Hindu sacred text? *How* is it used in services? *Why* is it important?

Answer the questions on page 32 about Hindu worship.

Muslim religious leaders

The leader of a Muslim community is known as the IMAM (see right).

These men are often also hafiz, which means that they know the QUR'AN by heart. Some have studied Islamic law (Shariah) in depth. All these facts make them highly respected. An imam must be of good character and well respected as an honourable Muslim. He leads services in the mosque, for example, during Friday prayer and Ramadan. He also supports the community by giving advice or acting on religious matters, such as divorce.

A symbol of Islam

The symbol for Islam is a crescent moon and five-pointed star. These can be seen on the minarets on every mosque. When the prophet MUHAMMAD 🕌 was alive, men used the moon and stars to help them find their way when travelling. In the same way, the moon and stars remind the worshipper that Allah is their guide. The star's five points represent the Five Pillars of Islam, which are duties that all Muslims must keep.

Muslim sacred writings

The Qur'an (see left), meaning recitation, is the sacred text of Islam. Angel Jibril gave the text to the prophet Muhammad 🕌, direct from Allah. Muslims say it is the word of Allah. It tells them about Allah and gives them rules by which they must live their lives if they want to go to paradise (heaven). It is treated with great respect. For example, it is never placed directly onto the floor and worshippers wash before reading it.

Revision tip

Have you tried using different coloured pens for your two religions? It will help to remember them separately because of the colour link, so that you won't mix up the religions in the exam. Some religions have a colour associated with them, like Islam and green.

Answer the questions on page 32 about Islamic worship.

Looking inside a Muslim mosque

The photos above and on the right are the outside and the inside of different Muslim mosques.

The **QIBLAH WALL** represents the direction to the Ka'bah (the sacred pilgrim shrine) in the city of Makkah. Muslims must face the Ka'bah when they pray. QIBLAH is actually the direction for prayer, not the wall. The wall may be plain, but often has beautiful geometrical patterns on it or Islamic calligraphy. Making these is a form of worship, but they also inspire the worshippers in their prayer.

The **MIHRAB** is the focus of the qiblah wall and represents the actual Ka'bah. It is often

an alcove in the wall and the most highly-decorated part of the whole wall. Decorations are usually sections of the Qur'an, written in calligraphic style. Geometric patterns are also used. The mihrab also amplifies the imam's voice as he speaks.

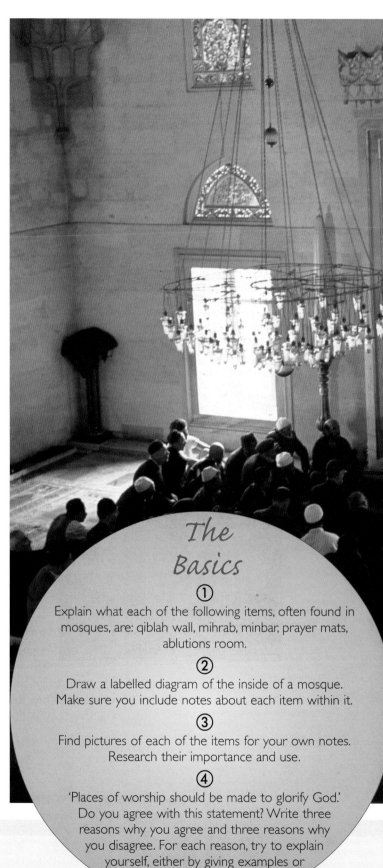

The Basics

① Explain what each of the following items, often found in mosques, are: qiblah wall, mihrab, minbar, prayer mats, ablutions room.

② Draw a labelled diagram of the inside of a mosque. Make sure you include notes about each item within it.

③ Find pictures of each of the items for your own notes. Research their importance and use.

④ 'Places of worship should be made to glorify God.' Do you agree with this statement? Write three reasons why you agree and three reasons why you disagree. For each reason, try to explain yourself, either by giving examples or by writing more fully.

The **MINBAR** is a platform for the imam to stand on when he is preaching the khutbah (sermon) to the worshippers at Friday prayer. It is usually to the right of the mihrab. It ensures that he can be seen and heard by all. People have to look up to see and hear him as he speaks from the Qur'an. This shows their respect for the word of Allah. A minbar is usually like a small staircase, but many mosques now have a podium instead.

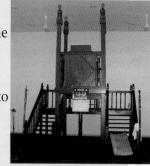

The carpet may have a **PRAYER MAT** design or be made of many prayer mats. The patterns or images of mosques on them can inspire the worshipper. They help Muslims to position themselves properly for prayer, and also make it more comfortable to sit or kneel.

There may be a **PRAYER NOTICE** that shows the five prayer times for that day. Every day these times will be slightly adjusted because the amount of daylight changes every day of the year. Muhammad ﷺ gave set times for prayer, and Muslims need to know those times in order to be able to pray correctly.

Muslims must be ritually clean before prayer, so every mosque will have an **ABLUTIONS ROOM**. Muslims follow a set routine when washing (called wudu).

Every mosque has a **WOMEN'S WORSHIPPING AREA**. Women do not have to go to the mosque – unlike men. If they do go, they have their own area so that their modesty is protected.

Worship in Islam

A Muslim girl prays at home.

Muslim prayer

Worship is central to Islam and can be performed in many ways. Prayer, or SALAH, is one of the Five Pillars of Islam – the five duties that all Muslims must carry out. All Muslims have to pray five times every day, in a set manner, at set times, and at the mosque if possible. Before they pray, they must be ritually clean and so they wash. This is called wudu.

The Prophet, Muhammad ﷺ, taught Muslims how to pray. Praying is done through a series of actions called a rak'ah. These involve bowing and prostrating, while saying parts of the Qur'an. Muslims copy Muhammad's ﷺ actions for the same number of times each day, but do more rak'ah each time.

Mosques have a caller, called a muezzin, who calls the adhan (prayer call). This alerts people that it is time to pray. Having carried out the ritual wash, they enter the prayer room. They stand facing the qiblah wall and begin to pray. Worshippers will make as many rak'ah as they feel they need to, on top of a compulsory number for each prayer time. Most prayer is done individually. However, on Friday, which is the holy day for Muslims, all adult males should go to the mosque for Friday prayer (jumu'ah) around midday. It is a duty. They will do the rak'ah together as one big group, and will then stay to listen to a sermon given by the imam. Afterwards, they can stay to ask questions to the imam about his sermon or teachings or ask for other advice, before returning home. Some women will attend this prayer, but most stay at home. Muslim women have to pray, but not at the mosque.

Prayers at home

Prayer at home is similar to that carried out in the mosque. A clean area is used – often the same area each time, as if a kind of mosque is created in the home. Some type of symbol will mark the direction of Makkah. Often it is a piece of calligraphy or a picture of the Great Mosque at Makkah. Prayer mats, on which worship takes place, will be placed to face Makkah. There won't be a sermon at home but it is possible to watch the sermon on television on Friday afternoon.

The prayers are spaced evenly throughout the day, so that Muslims have to focus regularly on Allah. They are encouraged also to think of Allah as often as they can during the non-prayer times. Thinking of Allah stops the mind thinking unholy thoughts instead, and so helps Muslims to remain pure and good.

So why do Muslims pray?

For a Muslim, salah (prayer) is a duty. Not praying will lead to punishment on Judgement Day. It is also a way to focus on Allah and connects worshippers to other Muslims. This sense of community (ummah) has been very important in Islam since the beginning of the religion, as it ensures Islam continues.

Aids to worship

In the mosque, the mihrab helps the worshipper to focus on Allah and the religion. Being able to read and understand the calligraphy is a reminder of the nature of Allah. Using prayer beads (TASBI) can also help concentration, as prayers or short Qur'anic phrases are chanted while holding each bead. Another aid to worship is the prayer mat, which is often decorated with an image of a famous mosque or the Ka'bah. It represents a clean, holy place to pray and the images on the mat are inspirational.

Muslims attending Jumu'ah prayer at the mosque.

They face Makkah to pray.

Each Muslim will complete many rak'ah as they pray.

Muslims use prayer beads called tasbi.

The imam gives a sermon to the whole congregation.

Research Task –

Find some different prayer mat designs. What symbols do you see in them?

How are prayer mats used by Muslims?

Use these pictures to remember the details of Muslim worship. Describe what you see and you will have a good idea of the main elements of a service.

Looking inside a Jewish synagogue

The photos above and on the right are the outside and inside of different Jewish synagogues.

NER TAMID is a light that is always kept alight. It represents the everlasting light of God. It is always at the front of the synagogue.

The **ARK OF THE COVENANT** (*Aron Hakodesh* in Hebrew) is the cupboard in which the TORAH SCROLLS are kept, when not in use during a service. It is always at the front of the synagogue in the centre, so worshippers look towards it. It is the holiest part of the synagogue, reminding everyone of the covenant with God upon which Judaism is based. It represents the Holy of Holies, which was the part of the Temple in Jerusalem where only the priests could go. A screen, called the *parochet*, covers the ARK.

In Orthodox synagogues, the **SEATING** is split into separate sections for men and women to make sure the focus is on God, not each other. In Reform synagogues, both sexes sit together.

The **BIMAH** is a raised platform at the front or in the middle of a synagogue. The Torah scrolls are placed onto a reading desk here and read during services. The platform is raised, which shows respect to the words of the Torah.

The **TORAH SCROLLS** are the sacred writings of Judaism. They are stored in the ark when not in use and are kept in decorated covers.

The **MENORAH** and the **TEN COMMANDMENTS** are two of the most important symbols of Judaism. The menorah (seven-branched candlestick) reminds Jewish people of God as the creator of all. When the Temple existed in Jerusalem, the MENORAH was always alight, representing God (doing the job that Ner Tamid does now). The TEN COMMANDMENTS are the most important rules given by God to Moses on Mount Sinai.

The **RABBI'S SEAT** is at the front of the synagogue and is reserved for the RABBI. He sits here during the service. He will stand near this seat to give a sermon or there may be a pulpit for this purpose next to the ark. Opposite or nearby is a second seat for the chazzan, who leads the hymns, readings and prayers.

The Basics

①

Explain what each of the following items, often found in synagogues, are: Ner Tamid, menorah, ark of the covenant, Torah scrolls, bimah.

②

Draw a labelled diagram of the inside of a synagogue. Make sure you include notes about each item within it.

③

Find pictures of each of the items for your own notes. Research their importance and use.

④

'Religious people need places of worship.' Do you agree with this statement? Write three reasons why you agree and three reasons why you disagree. For each reason, try to explain yourself, either by giving examples or by writing more fully.

Worship in Judaism

Worship at the synagogue

Prayer is central to a Jewish act of worship. As a duty, all Jews pray three times a day. Some will try to go to the synagogue to pray with others because, in Judaism, public prayer is seen as more important than private prayer. The most important Jewish prayers can only be said by a group of at least ten adults (minyan), who must all be male in Orthodox Judaism. On Monday, Thursday and Shabbat (Friday evening to Saturday afternoon), the Torah is read as part of the services. The service is always read in Hebrew and follows the siddur (prayer book) order. Worshippers attend the synagogue service, which may be led by a rabbi, but need not be. People often wear prayer shawls and other symbols of their religion.

The Saturday morning Shabbat service contains five sets of prayers, all spoken aloud in Hebrew. These include the Shema (declaration of faith), Amidah (eighteen blessings) and the Kaddish (end of service). The Torah scrolls are removed from the ark at the front of the synagogue, and paraded around the main area. Everyone stands as a sign of respect and some will try to touch the scrolls with their prayer shawl. The scrolls are taken to the bimah and placed on the lectern, where someone reads from them. Each service has a fixed portion of the Torah to be read, so everyone knows what to expect. Someone else will read a second section, but from the Neviim (Book of Prophets). There is singing of hymns and psalms, accompanied, in some synagogues, by music led by the chazzan. Shabbat services often include a sermon from the rabbi who tries to help the congregation understand the reading, but he may also talk about a current issue for the community. After the service, it is usual for the congregation to have a little to eat and drink.

The Torah is taken out of the Ark and paraded around the synagogue.

A member of the congregation reads from the Torah.

The rabbi gives a sermon.

Jews praying during worship in the synagogue.

Use these pictures to remember the details of Jewish worship. Describe what you see and you will have a good idea of the main elements of a service.

All Jews pray individually at certain times. When they pray, they wash and dress to show that they are fit to worship. The times for prayer are set within blocks in the day as a reminder that Abraham prayed at the start of the day, Isaac in the middle and Jacob at the end of the day. This is a reminder to all Jews of the beginnings of the faith.

So why do Jews pray?

Prayer is a part of being Jewish. It is important to show devotion to God by following his rules, and by worshipping him. The whole Shabbat time is one of rest and religious study, remembering the rest day after the creation. So prayer on this day honours the Shabbat. All Jews perform prayer in the same traditional way, so it is a link to everyone in the faith and gives a sense of community. Jews also see prayer as a time when God can judge the intentions of the person praying.

Aids to worship

Jewish men wear special items of clothing when praying – a tallit (prayer shawl), two tefillin (leather boxes containing writing from the Torah) and a yarmulkah (skull cap). These remind them of the seriousness of what they are doing. Putting on the tefillin helps a Jew to focus on the prayer ahead, as it has to be worn in a special way. The positioning of the tefillin reminds a Jew that they must love and think of God. In a synagogue, there will be lots of images to remind them of God and their faith – the menorah, Torah scrolls or the Ten Commandments. If you were to watch a service, you'd see people performing certain movements, like covering their eyes for the first part of the Shema, or swaying when praying. These are traditions in Judaism and linked to readings from the Torah and Talmud (the book of Jewish law). The swaying represents the flickering flame of a candle, which is said to flicker in harmony with the Torah. It shows that the worshipper is trying to be in harmony with the Torah.

An orthodox Jewish man at prayer. His tallit and tefillin are visible.

Research Task —

Find out about the meal and rituals that begin or end Shabbat in the home. What are they? What do they symbolise?

Jewish religious leaders

The word rabbi means 'my master' and shows how much they are respected. Rabbis (see right) have had formal training on the Torah and Talmud, often obtaining a degree, and so are experts in Jewish scripture and law. Originally, this was the focus of being a rabbi and many did not even work in synagogues. Today, most rabbis work in their community doing pastoral work, providing support and guidance to the members of their synagogue and teaching the religion.

Jewish sacred writings

The Tenakh is the name for the three sections of sacred writings that Jews use. The most important of the three is the Torah, said to be the word of God which was given to Moses by God. It is hand-written in Hebrew and found in scroll form in every synagogue (see right). The other two sections are the Neviim (Book of Prophets) and the Ketuvim (writings).

A symbol of Judaism

The menorah (see above) is the most common symbol of Judaism. It originally stood in the temple to represent God and was always lit, showing that God lasts forever. Now the menorah stands at the front of each synagogue, with Ner Tamid, representing God. The seven branches of the menorah represent the seven days of creation.

Revision tip

Make a set of flashcards and get someone to test your knowledge regularly with them. Put images and words onto the cards for each of your religions. When someone shows you one, talk about it. For example, in Judaism use words and images of Ner Tamid, the menorah symbol and so on.

Answer the questions on page 32 about Jewish worship.

Sikh religious leaders

An elected committee of people manage the Sikh GURDWARAS. This committee is newly elected every year. Some gurdwaras have a permanent GRANTHI (see left) – a person who can read the GURU GRANTH SAHIB clearly and correctly. This person is the leader of the community and in Britain they also do a lot of pastoral work in the community. The Granthi leads services, but is helped by others (anyone competent can read the Guru Granth Sahib). Musicians (ragis) sing and play devotional music to help the congregation understand its teachings. All of these people are respected within the community for the devotion they show to the Guru Granth Sahib and the religion.

Revision tip

Get pictures of as many of the things you study as you can. A picture with a label on it sticks better in many people's heads than just writing. Then you can think of the image in the exam to help you remember. For example, find an image of the Sikh Khanda and label it.

A symbol of Sikhism

The KHANDA symbol (see right) is made up of a circle (chakra). This represents God who is everlasting, because a circle has no beginning and no end. It is also like a boundary, showing that Sikhs must keep within God's rule. The two swords, or kirpans, are symbols of spiritual and political power and remind Sikhs that they must fight for truth. The double-edged blade is called a khanda – the name for the symbol. It represents God.

Sikh sacred writings

The most sacred text for Sikhs is called the Guru Granth Sahib (see above), made up of poems and hymns written by Guru Nanak and other Sikh Gurus. It was put together by Guru Gobind Singh, who said that it would be the final Guru of the Sikh faith – an eternal and unchanging Guru. Copies are made but they must be exactly the same as the original. Most copies are found in gurdwaras, where they are sometimes given their own room when not being used in a service. This is an example of the great respect shown to this sacred text.

Answer the questions on page 32 about Sikh worship.

Looking inside a Sikh gurdwara

The photos above and on the right are the outside and the inside of different Sikh gurdwaras.

The **GURU GRANTH SAHIB** is the holy book of Sikhism, made up of hymns written by the Gurus. Any building that contains a Guru Granth Sahib can be classed as a gurdwara.

The **PALKI** is a throne made of cushions. The Guru Granth Sahib is placed on the PALKI to be read. The **TAKHT** is the canopy that stands over the throne. They are found at the front of the gurdwara in the middle of the prayer hall. Traditionally, an umbrella shaded the honoured guests in India and so the TAKHT represents this symbol of respect. The palki raises the Guru Granth Sahib off the ground. Sikhs sit on the floor during the service so they have to look up to the Guru Granth Sahib and the Granthi who is reading. This shows both respect and humility. Since everyone sits on the floor, this also shows equality between all people.

The Basics

①

Explain what each of the following items, often found in gurdwaras, are: palki, takht, Mool Mantra, offerings, Guru Granth Sahib.

②

Draw a labelled diagram of the inside of a gurdwara. Make sure you include notes about each item within it.

③

Find pictures of each of the items for your own notes. Research their importance and use.

④

'Anyone can worship anywhere.' Do you agree with this statement? Write three reasons why you agree and three reasons why you disagree. For each reason, try to explain yourself, either by giving examples or by writing more fully.

The **MOOL MANTRA** is the statement of belief in one God, which was first made by Guru Nanak. Its words describe God. It is usually clearly displayed at the front of the prayer hall.

PICTURES OF SPIRITUAL LEADERS adorn the walls. These are usually Sikh Gurus, but may include pictures of the spiritual leaders of other faiths too, like Muhammad , Jesus or the Buddha – leaders who showed the path to God and are inspirational to the worshippers.

When Sikhs enter the gurdwara, they bring **OFFERINGS** of food, flowers or money. These are given at the front of the prayer hall before the worshipper sits down for the service. The food will be used in the LANGAR meal for the community.

A group of **MUSICIANS** (ragis) play music throughout the service. Their songs help the worshippers to understand the message of the Guru Granth Sahib and inspire them to think of God.

There is a **RESTING PLACE** for the Guru Granth Sahib. When not being used in a service, the Guru Granth Sahib has to be kept in its own room. It is shown the respect a human Guru would be shown. There it is covered by romallas (fine clothes made or given by the worshippers).

Each gurdwara has **KITCHENS** to provide a free meal to anyone who has attended or comes to the gurdwara. This practice was started by Guru Nanak at Kartarpur to feed those who had travelled long distances. It is a symbol of the duty of sewa (service) that all Sikhs must carry out. The meal is eaten in the langar (communal kitchen).

Worship in Sikhism

Worship at the gurdwara

The Sikh holy day is Sunday. Most Sikhs will attend the gurdwara for a part of the service. When Sikhs go to the gurdwara, they will already have made sure they are clean. Outward cleanliness represents inward godliness in many religions. They take off their shoes and cover their heads before entering the main hall. Then, they will go straight to the front of the hall and make an offering to the Guru Granth Sahib of flowers, food or money. They prostrate before the Guru Granth Sahib and then sit down.

The Guru Granth Sahib will have been brought from its room to the takht earlier in the morning. It is carried above someone's head, while everyone in the room stands. A person walks ahead of it, sprinkling amrit (holy water) onto the floor. It is placed on the takht and opened at any page to be read. The first reading will be used as the main reading of the day and is written onto boards for all to see, as well as re-read many times.

The service is called DIWAN and can last many hours, so people are expected to come and go as they wish. A Granthi reads from the Guru Granth Sahib, and musicians (ragis) play music and sing hymns to help the worshippers understand the meaning of the readings. This is called kirtan. There will also be some spoken explanations of the teachings. Not everyone can understand the language of the Guru Granth Sahib and, even if they can, its meaning may not be as clear as they need it to be. The musical and spoken explanations are a great help in understanding how to live properly as a Sikh. During the service, a simple food called karah parshad is made and given out to the worshippers. Everyone has some food, which is a way of showing that all people are equal.

When people have decided that they have spent enough time in the service, they leave the main hall and go to eat at the langar. Guru Nanak set up the idea of giving food to those who had travelled to worship, while Guru Amar Das made it a rule that Sikhs eat at the langar before speaking to him. So eating at the langar has become a tradition, and every gurdwara is built with kitchens for this very reason. Each week, the langar will provide a full VEGETARIAN meal for all of the worshippers, paid for by the community as part of the Sikh duty of service (sewa). Everyone is welcome – Sikh and non-Sikh.

Sikhs are encouraged to focus on God as much as they can, so private prayer is very important. Many Sikhs meditate, some using prayer beads called mala to help them. Most Sikhs begin the day with prayer, then at dusk and before going to bed they repeat two specific hymns. They may study lavan (hymns from the Guru Granth Sahib) from a gutka (prayer book). Since the gurdwara is open every day, any Sikh can attend whenever they want to.

Sikhs eating together in the langar.

So why do Sikhs pray?

It is a Sikh duty to repeat the name of God (Nam Japo) or meditate on the name of God (Nam Simran). Both actions are seen as a way of purifying the soul. If a person always thinks of God, they can't be thinking of misbehaving or doing wrong. Sikhs believe in reincarnation and so they aim for a better rebirth – good behaviour is vital. Prayer is a way to understand the religion and its teachings more deeply. It is also a link to all Sikhs, back to the first Guru, and so has a sense of tradition, community and equality.

Aids to worship

Prayer beads help the worshipper to focus. The kirtan helps them to understand, and can also make it easier to pray or meditate. Wearing the 5KS (the five religious symbols of KHALSA Sikhs) is a visible reminder of the values that the religion is based upon. Although Sikhs don't usually have a copy of the Guru Granth Sahib, many have the gutka, which contains about twenty hymns.

When Sikhs enter the prayer hall, they make offerings to the Guru Granth Sahib.

The Granthi reads from the Guru Granth Sahib.

Ragis play music to help understand the teachings.

Sikh man wearing the 5Ks.

Sikhs praying.

Research Task —

Find out about the 5Ks — what are they? What does each stand for?

Use these pictures to remember the details of Sikh worship. Describe what you see and you will have a good idea of the main elements of a service.

What do you know about worship?

The questions on this page are designed to give you a set of notes for each of the two religions you are studying. Think of how you can make the two sets of notes distinct – use different colours of writing, or use different exercise books, or use the front and back halves of your exercise book. It helps to have a clear split between the two religions, as this should help you both to remember and revise.

This page contains a set of research questions too. This extends the information you have and will definitely improve your overall understanding.

Try to get pictures of examples of everything – have a visual reminder of what you have studied, as well as a written one.

Answer these questions clearly and in full sentences so that when you read it later, it will all make sense. If it doesn't, you won't be able to revise from it.

1. Draw the symbol and explain what it stands for.

2. Name a religious leader. Why is this leader important?

3. Name the holy book. Why is it important?

4. How do worshippers show their respect for their holy book?

5. Describe an act of worship at the place of worship.

6. Describe an act of worship at home (if the answer to this isn't obvious, say what a worshipper could do at home to worship God).

7. Choose two elements of an act of worship, and explain the importance and symbolism of each.

8. Describe how worshippers pray and/or meditate.

9. Why are prayer and/or meditation important?

10. What aids to worship can be used? How do they help in worship?

Research Task –

Use research to find out:

✓ Another symbol and its meaning.

✓ Where you can take a virtual tour of a place of worship, then take it.

✓ If there are any other acts of worship that take place, for example, at a festival.

✓ More about meditation, including mysticism.

✓ More of the range of religious leaders, their jobs and the differences between them.

✓ More about the holy book, including other holy books.

✓ More detail about the aids to worship.

Exam Tips

Everybody wants to know what is on the exam paper – that way you could learn just the right bits and not waste time revising anything else. But no one can tell you what is in the exam. You could guess the areas of questions by working out what was on the last few exam papers, and looking for gaps or patterns. The exam paper has to be a fair reflection of the specification over time, so it can't ignore one bit of a topic for years and years.

In this subject, all the questions have to be answerable from all six religions. This means it can't ask you what a certain word means, for example, *diwan*, or anything specific to a religion, such as *why communion is important*. If the paper asked those sorts of questions, anyone who hadn't studied Christianity and Sikhism wouldn't be able to answer all the questions. The exam paper would be unfair. So, questions will be written in a way that allows an answer from all of the six religions, like these:

1 Name the place of worship for each of the two religions you have studied.

2 Describe an act of worship for each of the religions you have studied.

3 Name two of the furnishings in a place of worship and explain their importance for each of the religions you have studied.

Have a look at these questions – they couldn't be asked in an exam. Can you make them into general questions that could be asked?

1 Describe the outside of a mosque.

2 Name the Buddhist holy book.

3 Why is worship important in Hinduism?

4 Explain why the rabbi is important in Judaism.

5 Name an object Christians use as an aid to worship and explain it.

Think of a set of questions that could be asked in the exam and that you could answer from both of your chosen religions. Write them down and swap with a partner. Answer each other's questions.

Answering evaluative questions well

There will be four of these for you to answer on the paper. Each is worth five marks, giving a quarter of the total mark for the paper. So, if you are good at these, you can really boost your grade. If not, you'll lose out.

You get the marks for doing two things – focusing on the statement that is given, and writing about it from two different sides.

It is easiest if you have a technique to follow, so try this:

Disagree with the statement

Reasons must be given for disagreeing

Explain those reasons

Agree with the statement

Reasons must be given for agreeing

Explain those reasons

If you try to remember DREARE, you can work out the rest and you will have a good answer every time.

So, how do you get the marks? There are five levels on offer:

LEVEL	CRITERIA	MARKS
Level 1	Just giving a reason, with no explanation, will get you…	… 1 mark
Level 2	Giving two or more reasons, with no explanations, will get you… Giving one reason and explaining it will also get you…	… 2 marks
Level 3	If your answer is one-sided, but you give a few reasons, and explain one or two of them, you'll get… Or if you try to answer from both sides, and give a bit of explanation, you'll probably get…	… 3 marks
Level 4	Your answer has to be two-sided and you have to give a few reasons on each side, with some explanation too. It also has to include some religious arguments, if you want to get…	… 4 marks
Level 5	Your answer has to be two-sided (or more) and you have to have a few reasons, with a lot of explanation. It also has to include some religious arguments, if you want to get…	… 5 marks

Spot the level

Read the answers to this question and decide which level they are using from that chart.

'Holy books are out of date and useless.' Do you agree? Give reasons for your answer, showing that you have thought about more than one point of view. (5 marks)

Answer one: I don't agree. The holy book is God's word and that lasts forever.

Answer two: I disagree in some ways. Holy books have been around a long time and most religious people think they still have a use today. If they are God's word, like Muslims claim, they must still be useful because his words last forever.
In other ways I agree. How many people use a holy book to tell them how to live their lives? How many holy books tell us about nuclear war, abortion, or whether genetic engineering is right? They don't, because those things weren't invented then.

The first answer has one reason – *what mark is it worth?*

The second answer has two sides. Each side has a couple of reasons, with a bit of explanation – *what mark is it worth?*

What could you do to each to improve those marks?

Try to practise some of these questions yourself. Use the technique and the chart to help you build up your answers.

1 'Places of worship cost too much.' Do you agree? Give reasons and explain your answer, showing that you have thought about more than one point of view.

2 'You should go to worship at a religious building every day if you are really religious.' Do you agree? Give reasons and explain your answer, showing that you have thought about more than one point of view.

3 'Religious leaders are the best guides to how God wants you to live your lives.' Do you agree? Give reasons and explain your answer, showing that you have thought about more than one point of view.

Common faults in the exam with evaluative questions

▸ Candidates don't read the statement properly, so they only answer a bit of it or they answer wrongly.

▸ Candidates answer from one point of view – they only agree or disagree.

▸ Candidates don't EXPLAIN their answer, even when they give lots of reasons.

The first fault can cost you all five marks. The second two will make it impossible to get more than 3 marks for the question – no matter how brilliant your answer is or how many reasons you give.

When you check your answer, do a technical check like this. The words in italics are what you should be thinking as you read the question.

Ok, let's see. 'Holy books are out of date.' *Did I answer that statement?* Do you agree? *Well, did I agree?* Explain your answer. *Did I give explanations?* And give reasons. *Have I given more than just one reason?* Showing that you have thought about more than one point of view. *Have I put two points of view?*

If you answer yes each time when you check your answer, you should be fine. If you found a bit you didn't do, you can add what is missing.

Basic values

All religions have basic values and principles, and this page picks out some of them. Not every value is listed, just the most obvious ones. These are useful for doing the exam, because if you know them, you can apply them to any issue or topic. Copy the text into the front of your exercise book or file and then use it as the basis for your work. When you study a topic, refer back to this list to help you to work out what the religious attitude may be to that topic.

Buddhism

1 Rebirth and karma – our words, thoughts and deeds create energies that shape future rebirths. We need to make sure these are positive.

2 The FIVE PRECEPTS or guidelines for living. These are: not harming others; using language kindly; not taking what is not freely given; not clouding our minds; no sexual misconduct.

3 COMPASSION (loving kindness) and ahimsa (non-violence).

Christianity

1 Jesus' two great commandments are to love God and to love your neighbour.

2 EQUALITY for all, because in Genesis we are told that God made each of us.

3 JUSTICE (fairness) – since everyone is equal, everyone deserves fairness.

4 Forgiveness and love are ideas taught and demonstrated by Jesus.

Hinduism

1 Ahimsa (non-violence)

2 Self-discipline

3 Tolerance

4 Service to others

5 Compassion

6 Providing shelter/support to others

7 Respect for all life

8 Wisdom

9 Honesty with others and oneself

10 Cleanliness

Islam

1 The UMMAH – brotherhood of all Muslims. This means that all Muslims are equal and deserve the same respect and treatment.

2 All are created equal, because God created all.

3 Everyone has to follow duties set by Allah (God), for example, the Five Pillars.

4 Shariah law, Muslim law stemming from the Qur'an and HADITH, is applied to modern life by Islamic scholars.

5 Islam means peace, and Muslims should try to promote peace.

Judaism

The Ten Commandments are found in the book of Genesis in the Torah.

1 Love only God.

2 Make no idols of God.

3 Do not take God's name in vain.

4 Keep the Sabbath holy.

5 Respect your parents.

6 Do not kill.

7 Do not steal.

8 Do not commit ADULTERY.

9 Do not tell lies.

10 Do not be jealous of what others have.

Sikhism

1 Meditation and service to the one God, including worship, following the teachings, and wearing the 5Ks as a mark of the faith and devotion to it.

2 Do not use intoxicants.

3 Do not eat meat that has been ritually slaughtered (most Sikhs are vegetarians).

4 Equality of all people, leading to respect for all and a desire to fight injustice, including not hurting others by theft or deed.

5 Ethical virtues such as sharing with others, dutifulness, prudence, justice, tolerance, temperance, chastity, patience, detachment and humility.

Research Task —

1 Find out more detail about the values and virtues of the two religions you have studied. See if you can locate some scriptural teachings for them, so that you can explain them more fully.

2 Find out some other values and virtues for your two religious traditions. You may be able to do this by interviewing a member of those faiths.

2 Protest, Pressure Groups and Minority Rights

Protest

This is actually the last unit in the specification, but there is a good reason to look at it now. The specification says that you can be asked about this topic in relation to any of the other topics, so you always have to be ready for a question. As you work through the other units, ask yourself if there is an organisation that fights for that issue and find out about it. *Protest Slots* and *Organisation Profiles* are placed in other units to give you an idea of a group linked to those issues.

Anti-abortion campaigners picket outside clinic

Thousand-page petition against lowering age of consent delivered to Downing Street

Animal rights protestors break into laboratories

Hyde Park anti-racist rally attended by thousands

Look at the headlines above. People PROTEST in many ways, about many things. They protest because they don't agree with an issue. Just one person could protest, but when lots of people protest, change can happen.

Many people believe that protest should be peaceful – in other words, it shouldn't lead to property damage or people getting hurt or killed. They believe they can cause change by the size and length of their protest, and eventually it will have an effect.

Some people believe that they have to use violence because they have failed to make change happen in any other way. For example, some animal rights protestors damaged laboratories where animal testing was being done, and a group of refugees sewed up their own eyes and mouths to publicise their fear of being deported back to their own countries.

> **Research Task –**
>
> For the next two weeks, keep an eye on the news — local, national and international. Find examples of how and why people have protested.

The Basics

①
Why do people protest?

②
How could people protest? Split your answer into protest by individuals and protest by groups.

③
Give some examples of things people might protest against.

④
'Protests are too easy to ignore, so they change nothing.' Do you agree with this statement? Give two reasons why you agree and explain them, then give two reasons why you disagree and explain them.

Definitions

Protest – public dissent against something and action to change it

Pressure groups – organisations formed to raise public awareness of an issue, who try to make change happen through their work

Minority rights – the belief that people from small groupings within society should receive the same rights and opportunities as everyone else

Civil disobedience – refusing to do as the Government asks as a sign of protest, for example, withholding taxes that would go to defence spending

Non-violent protest – protest that is not violent, for example, marches

tasks

① Pick out the different forms of protest from the headlines on page 38, and think of more of your own.

② Now pick out the focus of their protest.

Research Task —

Find out what the following organisations protest about: Greenpeace, Commission for Racial Equality, Stonewall, Life, Fawcett Society, and World Wildlife Fund. Choose one and find out the history of the organisation. Do an in-depth study of how and why it protests.

There are two key questions to be aware of for questions on protest. Firstly, does the religion ever protest? Do members of that faith see protest as an acceptable thing to do? Secondly, how do they protest? Do they always keep to non-violent protest?

Buddhism

Do Buddhists protest?

During the Vietnam War, Buddhists protested. One famous picture shows the extent of the protest – a monk set fire to himself so that he would burn to death. He had previously informed the world's press, so that they could tell the world about his protest.

Tibetan Buddhists have protested against what they see as the occupation of Tibet by China for many years. The DALAI LAMA heads the Tibetan government in exile, based in India. For more information, read about Tibetan support groups on the www.tibet.org website.

Why do Buddhists protest?

Protest against injustice can be seen as the positive side of the precept to 'not harm others'. It could also be judged as 'Right Speech' and 'Right Action' (two parts of the Noble Eightfold Path) because Buddhists are speaking out or acting against injustice. Since COMPASSION is central to Buddhism, trying to make change happen to improve things for other people can be seen as compassionate.

How do they protest?

The Dalai Lama speaks only of non-violence. He says that only when there is an atmosphere of mutual respect will peace and harmony flourish. The Buddhist beliefs mentioned before also direct Buddhists towards non-violent protest. Increasingly Buddhists are becoming involved in 'engaged' Buddhism – that is, trying to be politically active.

However, the Buddhist monk who burnt himself to death used a violent form of protest, even though it was against himself. Many Buddhists in Tibet now want to be able to protest violently, because they believe non-violence has not worked.

During the Vietnam war, a Buddhist monk set himself alight to get the world's attention about the suffering going on.

Christianity

Do Christians protest?

Christians believe in protest. For example, Martin Luther King, the Baptist minister who organised and controlled the American Black civil rights movement; Christians who protest outside ABORTION clinics; Jesus, who protested in the Temple in Jerusalem by turning over tables.

Christians are taught to fight injustice. The Gospel of Luke shows Jesus helping non-Jews and outcasts from society – it is often called the 'Gospel of the Underdog'.

Why do Christians protest?

In the earliest times of Christianity, Christians were a persecuted minority, so it seems natural that they would support MINORITY RIGHTS. The BIBLE says everyone is equal because God made us all. Therefore we should treat others as equals and make sure everyone has equal rights – this means protecting minority groups.

How do they protest?

Martin Luther King protested non-violently through marches, demonstrations, sit-ins and so on, believing that violence did not solve problems in the long-term and was not the Christian way. However, other Christians joined the Black Power movement, which encouraged violence because it could not see non-violence working quickly enough.

Jesus said 'Blessed are the peacemakers' in his sermon on the mount. He also told Christians to turn the other cheek in the face of violence and to love their enemies. These all suggest protest should be non-violent. Some Christians believe that sometimes violence is necessary as, without it, change cannot be forced and many people suffer for much longer. God gave us freedom of will and of choice. We have to use both responsibly but, ultimately, it is up to each of us to decide how to react.

Hinduism

Do Hindus protest?

Hindus believe in protest. Mahatma Gandhi led protests against British rule in India in the early twentieth century. He had already protested against apartheid in South Africa, and went on to protest for equal rights for all castes in India. As a committed Hindu, this was as much a religious act as anything else.

Why do Hindus protest?

The Hindu virtues of shelter and service to others should encourage any Hindu to protest where

they see injustice. Compassion and tolerance should help them to see the injustice in the first place and want to do something to change it.

How do they protest?

Gandhi believed only in non-violent protest because that was the sole way to achieve the goal correctly. The Arya Samaj is a group trying to break down caste barriers through making Untouchables (the lowest caste) a part of their society, and providing opportunities for them by treating them as equals. Their work is achieved through political pressure and non-violent means. All Hindus should follow ahimsa – non-violence.

Islam

Why do Muslims protest?

Muslims have a duty to fellow Muslims to support them, and this can mean protest. In the UK, we have seen Muslim-organised protests, for example, against racism and Islamophobia, and against the war in Iraq. Freedom of conscience and religion is part of the Islamic Declaration of Human Rights, and so is protection for non-Muslims in Muslim countries – where that is contravened Muslims should protest.

How do they protest?

Islam means peace. Muhammad ﷺ said all Muslims should be peaceful in their behaviour and that violence is forbidden except in self-defence. Islam allows anyone to protest against anything they feel is unfair or do not accept.

But that protest should not put someone's life at risk. Violence is always a last resort, but there is an acceptance that, if all else fails, violence can be used. Muslims are also expected to hit back when struck, as dictated in the QUR'AN. This means that violent harassment, for example, could be repaid with violence. As it is a Muslim's duty to fight oppression, we sometimes see extremists use violence in the name of Islam. One example was the Black Muslim movement, led by Malcolm X, which fought against racist violence in the USA in the 1960s. Another is the Palestinian struggle in Israel, where Palestinians use 'martyrdom operations' (suicide bombings) to try to force change.

Judaism

Do Jews protest?

Jewish people protest. A Jewish tradition is to protest against injustice and to work to make the world a better place. This is because Jews believe God put them on Earth as stewards over people and the world. There is a duty to support others, including through protest, because we are all made in God's image. The books of the Neviim describe many stories of prophets who protested loudly about the behaviour of nations, groups and individuals. It is a part of Jewish history.

How do Jews protest?

You may have seen Jewish protest marches and demonstrations on television – against anti-Semitism, against the events in Israel and against occupation and resettlement. Those protests are non-violent. The organisation, Jews for Global Justice (see www.SocialAction.com), uses direct action and civil disobedience in its protest.

Sikhism

Do Sikhs protest?

For Sikhs, it is important that people are not persecuted for their beliefs. Where they see this happening, they should act, which can involve protest. One of the key values for Sikhs is sewa – service to others. This should motivate them to protest where they see injustice. In early 2005, the British press reported Sikhs protesting against a theatre production which they said was unfair to their religion. Sikhs have also protested for many years in a bid to have a homeland country in the area of Punjab in India.

How do Sikhs protest?

Since one aim of Sikhism is not to harm others, protest will usually be peaceful. However, Sikhism is a warrior religion and some of its symbols contain swords. This shows the willingness of Sikhs to fight physically for justice and equality in certain circumstances. An example of violent protest was the assassination of Indira Gandhi (Indian Prime Minister) by one of her Sikh bodyguards. This was a result of actions against Sikhs at the Golden Temple of Amritsar.

The Basics

Answer each of these questions for each of the two religions you have studied.

①
Give two examples of protest by that religion.

②
What values make them protest? Use the basic virtues from pages 36–37 to help you with this.

③
In what ways might they protest?

④
Do they agree with non-violent protest? Explain your answer, and use the virtues from pages 36–37 again.

⑤
Answer this question **only once**: 'Protesting peacefully does nothing but give more time to the injustice you are protesting about'. Give three reasons why you agree with this statement and explain them. Give three reasons why you disagree and explain them. Make sure at least two of your reasons are linked to religious ideas.

Revision tip

When you've done a test, before it is marked, get your teacher to tell you exactly what they were giving marks for in each question and guess how much your answers are worth in marks.

Then compare your estimate with your real mark. This makes you analyse your work more carefully. It helps you to understand where you went wrong and how to improve.

Now you know about religious attitudes to protest.

Exam Tips

Focusing on minority rights

Questions on this topic either focus on a minority group, for example, religious people and their rights, or they ask generally about attitudes to a minority group. Although the question sounds hard, it is not really difficult, as you can answer in a general way.

> Explain the attitude of the two religions you have studied to minority groups. (8 marks)

Some pointers:

▸ We can start by making the general point that religions should defend and support the groups that they accept. For example, Christians might fight for the rights of refugees, because they are God's children.

▸ We can also say that religions shouldn't persecute the groups they don't accept. Some minority groups go against what some religions accept, for example, Muslim law says that homosexuality is wrong. Clearly, Muslims wouldn't defend the rights of homosexuals, but they shouldn't attack those people either.

▸ Then we can point to the values of the religion that would make them help and support others. These values are true for any group they are defending. Most religions believe in stewardship – the duty to look after the world and the people in it, either because God wants us to or as a safeguard for the future (good karma).

All religions believe in the sanctity of life – that life is special because God created it. Religions also believe in equality, because God created each of us. That equality means we have to help each other, and not persecute those who are different.

▸ Finally, we can apply those values to the issue. We can say that, since the religion believes in these morals, they should seek to help and support minority groups. This may include working for them or with them, and protesting on their behalf.

Check your notes or this book, and find the values for your two religions. Then write an answer to the question:

▸ In two separate parts – one for each religion.

▸ Give three ideas/values for each religion.

▸ Clearly apply those ideas/values to the issue, as a way of explaining their attitudes to minority groups.

Application of ideas

Always ask yourself – what does my answer mean for the issue in the question?

The best students manage to answer in this way. They don't just write a series of reasons or ideas that the religion teaches. They show why each value is relevant to the issue in the question. This makes their answer clear and completely relevant.

3 Prejudice and Discrimination

Definitions

Prejudice – when someone has an idea about something, before they find out about it properly. Often it is a negative idea. It is often wrong, because it isn't based on real evidence. We use the word to describe a person's dislike of certain other people, when they have no good reason. We usually talk about prejudice against religion, colour, nationality, age, gender, sexuality or appearance.

Discrimination – when we act on our prejudices. We treat someone differently because they are not the same as us or what we know. That different treatment could be either better or worse treatment than we normally give people.

For this unit, you have to:

- understand both these words – PREJUDICE and DISCRIMINATION.

- know the attitudes of the two religions you have studied to general prejudice and discrimination.

- know the different types of prejudice and the attitudes of the two religions to these issues – the exam could focus on RACISM, SEXISM, HOMOPHOBIA, AGEISM, or prejudice against minorities or religions.

Rugby is a man's sport

- know what two religious traditions think about being prejudiced, about discriminating against people, and how they fight prejudice.

- be able to say how individuals, groups, society and the law should respond to prejudice.

There are three key ideas that religious traditions base their attitudes on. These ideas are:

I don't allow white friends in my social group

Definitions

Equality – that everyone is as important or valuable as everyone else

Justice – that everyone has the same rights and deserves the same treatment

Community – that human beings are one big community, and so should help each other

Looking at prejudice and discrimination

Why are people prejudiced?

Everyone can be prejudiced at times, even by accident. Not everyone will discriminate against others because of prejudice.

People are prejudiced for many reasons. Here are three:

1 Having a bad experience with someone might make you think everybody is like that. For example, maybe when you were young, you were frightened by a grumpy old man. This makes you think all old men are grumpy.

2 Having always been told bad things about a certain group of people by parents, you might become prejudiced without even getting a chance to know any differently. Our upbringing has a big influence on us, and our parents' words have a huge effect.

3 Having seen something on television or read a newspaper that was very biased (it focused on only one fact or idea, taking it out of context), you might have believed it and so now have a prejudice.

It only takes someone to be different for them to be singled out for prejudice and discrimination. It might be because of how they look or behave, or maybe it is how someone else *thinks* they behave.

Look at what these people say. How could you challenge their prejudices?

Women should stay at home and tidy up the house.

Nadine

Two men holding hands – it's not natural!

Leeroy

Teenagers nowadays – they're all layabouts.

Jill

All fat people are lazy.

Uma

It's okay to pick on him, he's a swot!

Laura

Only men should drive buses.

Stu

The Basics

① Why do you think some people are prejudiced?

② How do some people discriminate against others?

③ List three types of prejudice. Give an example of each.

④ 'You can't stop people from being prejudiced.' Give three reasons why you agree and explain them. Now write three reasons why you disagree and explain them. You must use at least two religious ideas within your reasons.

Now you know about prejudice and discrimination.

Tackling questions on this topic

The exam can ask you general questions about this topic, such as: 'explain the attitudes to prejudice of the two religions you have studied.' It can also ask you specific questions, such as: 'explain the attitudes to racism of the two religions you have studied'. It could ask you a question that you don't even realise covers the same ground as this topic, such as: 'explain the attitudes to the rights of religious people of the two religions you have studied'. To answer any of these questions, you must study the beliefs for each religion concerning:

Equality

Justice

A sense of community

Sanctity of life

Loving kindness

If you learn the general ideas then you can apply them to the specific topics. Remember, religions don't agree with prejudice and discrimination because of all these beliefs/values.

BUDDHISM	CHRISTIANITY
1. Five Precepts – includes refrain from harming others; refrain from using language wrongly	1. The New Testament says love one another
2. Ahimsa – non-violence	2. New Testament – 'From one man he made every nation of men, that they should inhabit the whole earth …'
3. Metta – loving kindness (the Buddha said this should be shown to all beings)	3. Jesus helped anyone and was critical of those who excluded others
4. Anyone can join the Sangha – regardless of background	4. New Testament – 'So in everything, do to others what you would have them do to you …'
5. Unhelpful thoughts and desires – like being prejudiced, and discriminating – lead to bad karma. This affects our future rebirth.	5. Old Testament – 'So God created man, in his own image … male and female, he created them.'
6. The Dalai Lama, when asked what was the best way to live life, said, 'Always think compassion.'	6. In the Parable of the Good Samaritan, the man who was helped was helped because of his need, not because of who he was/was not

Read the columns that relate to the two religions you are studying. Make some notes. For each point, say what it relates to (fairness, equality, etc.). Now check back to page 36–37 for the general values of each religion you have studied. Add notes from there. Now you have enough detail to tackle any prejudice or discrimination question.

The Basics

①

Use your notes to write a paragraph about attitudes to prejudice for each of the two religions you are studying. Include and explain at least three ideas/teachings.

②

Use your notes to write a paragraph about attitudes to equality in each of the two religions you are studying.

three

HINDUISM	ISLAM	JUDAISM	SIKHISM
1. Ahimsa – non-violence, love and respect to all living beings 2. Bhagavad Gita – those who are sinless, have true wisdom and work for the welfare of all their fellow beings attain liberation 3. Compassion – a desire to improve things for others, not to persecute them 4. Respect for others, which leads to tolerance and support 5. Unhelpful thoughts and desires – like being prejudiced, and discriminating – lead to bad karma. This affects our future reincarnation. 6. Hindus have a duty to respect other faiths as alternative paths to the truth.	1. Muslim Declaration of Human Rights – All Muslims are equal 2. Qur'an – 'Let there be a community among you who will invite others to do good, command what is proper and forbid what is improper.' 3. Qur'an – 'Whenever you judge between people, you should judge with justice.' 4. Qur'an – 'You who believe, if some scoundrel should bring you a piece of news, clear up the facts lest you hurt some folk out of ignorance …' 5. Qur'an – 'God loves the fair-minded.' 6. Muhammad welcomed everyone, regardless of his or her colour or background.	1. Torah – 'When an alien lives with you in your land, do not ill-treat him … love him as yourself.' 2. The Seven Noachim Precepts are a set of rules for all men to live by. These include the promotion of justice. 3. Neviim – 'He has showed you, O man, what is good; and what does God require of you but to do justice, love kindness and walk humbly with your God?' 4. As early as the second century BC, Jewish leaders were saying that Jews and non-Jews should live in harmony, helping and accepting each other. 5. Torah – 'I will make you into a great nation, and I will bless you.' (The Hebrew word *goy* is used here, which includes anyone of any religion).	1. Adi Granth – 'Those who love God, love everybody.' 2. Mool mantra – 'This God is One … the Creator of all things.' 3. At a gurdwara, Sikhs hold the langar – community meal – after services. Everyone is welcome. 4. Adi Granth – 'Know people by the light that illuminates them, not by their caste.' 5. Akal Ustal – 'To recognise the oneness of all humanity is an essential pillar of Sikhism … humanity world-wide is made up of one race.' 6. At a service, anyone can read the Guru Granth Sahib, or can lead the service.

Now you know the religious teachings about prejudice.

three

Types of prejudice

The exam has asked specifically about racism and sexism in the past. However, it could ask you about any of the prejudices listed on the right. You already have a general response – that people are humans, life is sacred and it is important to uphold JUSTICE, EQUALITY and COMMUNITY. Therefore you can reasonably answer any question that comes up, as long as you remember these basic principles.

Look at the flowchart of ideas (Linking your Thinking) on the opposite page. Use the tasks below to guide yourself and a partner through it. You can use it as a revision guide too.

Thinking tasks – work with a partner on this.

1 *What types of prejudice are there? Give an example for each one.*

2 *How can each type of prejudice be fought? Are there some methods that are more effective than others for certain types of prejudice?*

3 *Which types of prejudice might a government get involved in trying to stop? Why and how?*

4 *How can we fight prejudice?*

5 *Split the ways in which we can fight prejudice into what individuals, groups/organisations, society and the law can do.*

6 *Which of the ways mentioned in question 5 – from individuals to the law – is the strongest? Why?*

7 *Do any of the ways to fight prejudice have any advantages over the others? What and why?*

8 *Why are people prejudiced?*

9 *How do people discriminate?*

10 *Do people discriminate in different ways for different types of prejudice? How and why?*

Definitions

There are lots of types of prejudice. This exam focuses on the ones below.

Racism – being prejudiced against someone because of the colour of their skin, or their nationality

Sexism – being prejudiced against someone because of their gender

Homophobia – being prejudiced against someone because they are homosexual or lesbian

Ageism – being prejudiced against someone because of their age

You can also be prejudiced against people because of their religion, either because it is different to yours or because you or they do not believe in religion.

Revision tip

Notice how the different areas of the topic are colour coded. This helps you to remember them. If you draw charts like this, as a memory aid, make sure you colour code them as well. You could put the completed ones on your bedroom wall at revision time, so they are all around for you to take in. In the exam, you can visualise them and their content on your walls.

11 What are the implications of the prejudice – for the victim and for society?

12 What are the religious attitudes of two religions to prejudice and/or discrimination?

13 Could prejudice or discrimination ever be justified? When?

14 What would you expect the attitudes of religions to be to each type of prejudice?

15 What might affect the attitude of a religion to one of those prejudices?

16 How do equality, justice and community link to each religion?

Linking your thinking

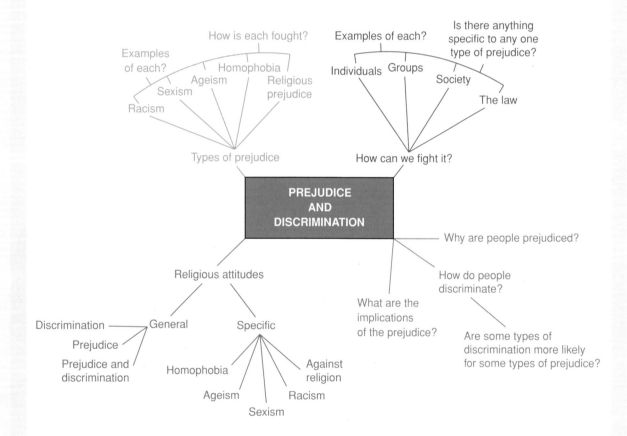

The next few pages look at the most common topics taken from this unit. You need to use the notes you made about general attitudes to prejudice (from pages 36–37 and 46–47), and add them to the specific issues that are described.

Racism

Definitions

Racism – the belief that the colour of a person's skin or their race affects their ability. It is also the belief that some races are better than others. We use the word 'racist' to describe someone who discriminates against people of other races in a negative way.

Racism is illegal. Most people think racism is wrong. Why should a person's skin colour or race make a difference? It shouldn't. If you are actively racist, you can pay a heavy price. You could lose your job, get expelled from school or go to prison.

Buddhism

Buddhists believe that we are all equal. By thinking of everyone else as equal, we break down the barriers to peace – we don't feel superior or look to outdo others, for example. The first step to seeing everyone as equal is to notice what everyone has in common. The DALAI LAMA once said that when he meets a person for the first time, he doesn't see them as male or female, American or Chinese, black or white, just human. The most basic thing about us all is that we are human. The idea of being superior or better is an illusion. Buddhists have to work to see things as they truly are. This is called Right Awareness. **Racism is wrong**.

Christianity

The Catholic Truth Society says 'Every human being is made in the image of God. We are all brothers, and neighbours of each other.' This statement underlines the fact that we are all equal and one big family. Families look after each other, rather than discriminate against each other. Also, there is the need to act on behalf of your faith, rather than simply agreeing with its principles, so Christians should actively fight prejudice. **Racism is wrong.**

Hinduism

All humans are equal in their search for liberation with the Supreme Reality (enlightenment), although each person is at their own stage in that search. Judging people based on their race is like judging people based on the car they drive or the clothes they wear. It is a false judgement and therefore unfair. Hindus believe your true self is the atman (soul), and as everyone has one, everyone is equal. **Racism is wrong.**

Islam

Prophet Muhammad ﷺ allowed a black African Muslim to make the call to prayer. When challenged, he pointed out that all men are equal, coming from one common ancestor and created by Allah.

Muslims believe that the colour of a person's skin or the country they were born in does not affect their standing before Allah. The differences in skin colour and language are meant to show the wonder of Allah's creation, not be a reason for discrimination. **Racism is wrong.**

Judaism

Nations have persecuted the Jews at numerous times throughout history. In the twentieth century, Nazi Germany tried to wipe out the Jews entirely. This was both religious and racial persecution. The TORAH tells Jews to welcome and not persecute strangers in their own land. Therefore, Jews must conclude that **racism is wrong**.

Sikhism

Sikhs believe that God has no colour or form, and God is the source of all life. To discriminate on the grounds of a person's colour or race is wrong. These are superficial judgements and Sikhs should look at the soul of an individual instead. Since Sikhs believe in REINCARNATION, behaving in a racist manner harms others and so adversely affects their rebirth. Sikhs strongly believe in fighting for justice and fighting against racism. **Racism is wrong.**

Fighting racism

Think back to all the ways that people protest. Religious people are no different and will use all those same ways – demonstrating, petitioning the government, issuing leaflets, holding rallies, marching, sit-ins and campaigns of civil disobedience. They also work together to support the victims of discrimination. As well as all of these methods, religious people pray – pray for strength, pray for help for those persecuted, and pray for ideas to stop the persecution.

Protest slot

Football Against Racism in Europe (FARE) is a European organisation devoted to ridding football of racism. FARE was set up in 1999 to bring together all the existing organisations in a Europe-wide network. Lots of top footballers from each country have become involved with FARE. Through activities such as tournaments, anti-racist matches, flyers at games, anti-racist T-shirts and much more, it aims to free football from racism. It also tries to promote racial harmony by helping mixed groups within football. For further information, see the website – www.farenet.org

Now you know about racism.

The Basics

① What is racism?

② How can people fight racism?

③ Explain the attitude of each of the two religions you have studied to racism. Use pages 36–37 and 46–47, as well as these pages to help you.

④ 'Racism is the worst kind of prejudice.' Do you agree with this statement? Give three reasons why you agree and three reasons why you disagree, including religious reasons.

Research Task —

Find out about the work of the CRE (Commission for Racial Equality).

Sexism

Sexism is prejudice because of someone's gender. It is about being unfair to someone because of their gender. Usually it is prejudice against women. Many religions see men's and women's roles as different, but they do not agree with gender prejudice and discrimination against women or men.

Some careers, such as working for the police, were traditionally considered male professions.

Buddhism

The Buddha allowed women to be ordained and said they could attain enlightenment just as men could. The Buddha can be seen in many forms, including female ones like Guanyin, the main form in China. Buddhism focuses on attaining enlightenment and discriminating against anyone would affect that goal.

There are a growing number of female teams in previously male-dominated sports, like rugby.

Christianity

Traditionally, men and women have had equal but different roles. However, in some branches of the Christian faith, women cannot become religious leaders. Women cannot become priests in either the Catholic or Orthodox traditions because of the tradition of male leaders started by Jesus. In other branches, such as Protestant groups, women can hold positions in the same way as men. They will be trained for leadership roles and judged on their suitability, not their gender.

A woman serving in the army.

Hinduism

Most BRAHMIN PRIESTS are male; only ISKCON (Krishna Consciousness Movement) has women priests. This is a reflection of the male-dominated society from which Hinduism comes, in which women manage the house while men bring in the income. Women are to be protected by their father, then their husband and finally their eldest son. There are several religious rituals that women cannot go through, including the Sacred Thread Ceremony. In India, there is evidence of discrimination against women through the high ABORTION rate of female foetuses, which is much above that of male foetuses. However, as India develops, the situation is changing.

In the UK today, women often work while raising a family.

Islam

The roles of men and women differ, but are equal. Muhammad ﷺ gave rights to women in Islam's earliest days, which helped them to have a higher position in society. Women have charge of the house, while men should protect women and bring in money for their family. Women also have the right to work if they wish. Both sexes should keep the rules of the Five Pillars.

Judaism

Progressive Judaism gives full equality to women in all religious matters, including divorce, and they can even be trained as RABBIS. Orthodox Judaism retains some religious laws that seem to question that equality – such as divorce, which only men can ask for. Men and women are equal but different, with separate roles, splitting the home (women) and the outside world (men).

Sikhism

'We are conceived and born from women. Woman is our life-long friend and keeps the race going. Why should we despise her, the one who gives birth to great men?' By saying this, Guru Nanak showed that men and women are equal, and that discrimination is wrong.

Fighting sexism

Religions can fight sexism by treating men and women equally and by not allowing sexist attitudes to pass unchecked. Within religions, setting an example of fairness is very important in establishing equality. Many religious groups have joined in demonstrations and campaigned to stop discrimination against women.

Protest slot

The FAWCETT SOCIETY (www.fawcettsociety.org.uk) was founded in 1953, originating from the National Union of Women's Suffrage Societies. It was named after a suffragette – Millicent Fawcett. It is the UK's leading organisation campaigning for equality between men and women.

The Fawcett Society focuses its work especially in political and economic fields, trying to raise public understanding of the position of women in society and helping women to take better advantage of political, economic and other opportunities. Its work includes funding research, campaigning politically and using the media to raise awareness of inequality issues.

The Basics

① What is sexism?

② How can sexism be fought?

③ Explain the attitude of each of the two religions you have studied to women (including their roles) and sexism.

Research Task –

Find out the arguments for and against having women as priests or religious leaders. Try to work out how much of each argument comes from culture, and how much from religious teachings. Write a conclusion based on your findings.

Now you know about sexism.

Ageism

All religions are concerned with the needs of the elderly.

This is discrimination against a person because of their age. It might have happened to you – have you ever been refused entry to somewhere or have people said you were too young to have an opinion on something? Usually we mean discrimination against older people, such as expecting them not to be fit enough to do a job or not to have relevant views on modern events.

Can you think of some different ways in which older and younger people are discriminated against?

Why do you think some people discriminate against those who are older or younger?

All religions believe in respecting the elderly. Elderly people attend places of worship more regularly than young people, mainly because they have more spare time to focus on worship and the church community. Committees that run places of worship include more older people than young ones. In some religions, old age is when you devote your thoughts and life to God/worship.

Now you know about ageism.

Of course, the religions all teach about equality and the importance of each individual. Both these ideas count for everyone, regardless of their age. You can check back to pages 46–47 for quotations from your religion on those ideas. You can also check pages 36–37 for the values of your religions.

WHAT RELIGIONS TEACH:	
Buddhism	Have respect for and be generous to others (Five Precepts).
Christianity	The Ten Commandments say respect your father and mother.
Hinduism	In Hindu society, the old are believed to be wise. Many men will focus on religion in old age and gain respect from that.
Islam	In Islamic society the old are believed to have wisdom, so should be respected.
Judaism	The Torah says respect your father and mother.
Sikhism	Sikhs believe in the wisdom of elders, and that this makes them deserving of respect.

The Basics

①
What do we mean by ageism?

②
How might people discriminate against a person because of their age?

③
Explain the attitude to ageism of the two religions you have studied. Use pages 36–37 and 46–47 so that you can include beliefs and teachings in your answer.

④
'The opinions of the young or old don't matter nowadays.' Do you agree with this statement? Give three reasons why you agree and explain them. Then give three reasons why you disagree and explain them. You must give at least one religious reason or argument in those reasons.

Homophobia

This is prejudice against people who are attracted to people of the same gender as themselves. Homophobia is different to the other prejudices. Religions accept without question someone's age, race or gender – however, they usually don't agree with homosexuality. If they do accept homosexuals, they usually disagree with gay sex. This means that even though they don't persecute homosexuals, they don't necessarily welcome them either.

In Britain, same sex couples can register legally as couples. This isn't the same as getting married, but it does mean that the law protects them and gives them certain rights. For example, they can get pension, inheritance and other rights that married couples get automatically.

Some people think that sex between two men or two women is unnatural and wrong. This is usually because it is impossible for this kind of sex to lead to children. It is also the case that there are quotations against homosexuality in the holy books. Homosexuals and lesbians can face lots of prejudice and are discriminated against because people do not agree with their relationships. Victims of other types of discrimination, such as racism, can get support from their families, who may have suffered similar experiences. For lesbians and homosexuals their families sometimes do not know they are gay or may even discriminate against homosexuals themselves. It can be very difficult for young people who work out they are gay and need to turn to their families.

Graham Norton.

Ellen DeGeneres and Portia de Rossi.

Revision tip

When you answer questions on religious attitudes to homophobia, remember to mention equality, justice, sanctity of life, and so on. Write about how these values should affect attitudes.

Now you know about homophobia.

The Basics

① What is homophobia?

② Why are people homophobic?

③ Explain the religious attitude to homophobia in each of the two religions you have studied. Use beliefs and teachings to develop your answer. Use pages 36–37 and 46–47 to help with values and general attitudes. Use pages 59–63 for specific religious attitudes.

④ 'Homosexuals are still God's children, so should have the support of religions like anyone else has.' Do you agree with this statement? Give two reasons why you agree and explain them. Then give two reasons why you disagree and explain them.

Exam Tips

According to the course specification, you need to know why people are prejudiced; how they show that prejudice; different forms of prejudice; what the attitudes of two religions are to prejudice generally (especially in relation to the concepts of justice, equality and community) and what the attitudes of two religions are to specific forms of prejudice. Do you know all these?

Try these questions. There are some tips on answering each. Use this book, or your notes, to help you.

1 Choose two different religious traditions and outline the teaching of each about prejudice and discrimination. (8 marks)

State the traditions, use quotations, explain the teachings. Try to make sure you use two quotes or teachings for each tradition. Refer back to pages 36–37 and 44–49.

2 How do people in one religious tradition apply their beliefs about prejudice and discrimination in practical ways? (6 marks)

In other words, what can people do to fight prejudice and discrimination, since they all disagree with it? Write down ways in which an individual could act, how a group could act, or what a religious group could do. Think about behaviour, speech and attitudes. This GCSE is about religion so make sure to include some religious elements in it.

3 'By sending their children to religious schools, some religious believers are encouraging them to be prejudiced against others.' Do you agree with this statement? Give reasons why you agree, showing you have thought about more than one point of view. (5 marks)

Remember to argue from two sides, agreeing and disagreeing. Give more than one reason for each side. Explain every reason you give and, if possible, also give examples as further explanation.

Time Test:

For this set of questions, give yourself 25 minutes and use no books.

1. *Explain, using examples, the difference between prejudice and discrimination. (4 marks)*

2. *What teaching is given about prejudice and discrimination in each of the two religions you have studied? (7 marks)*

3. *Describe how the teachings you have outlined in Question 2 are put into practice in this tradition with regard to people of different races. (4 marks)*

4. *An Anglican bishop has argued that it is not always wrong to discriminate against other people; it depends on the circumstances. Do you agree with his view? Give reasons for your opinion, showing that you have thought about more than one point of view. (5 marks)*

three

4 Human Sexuality, Issues and Relationships

This unit combines three areas from the specification – Human Sexuality and Sexual Relationships, Married and Family Life and Issues in Human Relationships. The exam paper could include several questions from these three sections, and often combines parts of each in any one question.

Sexuality

Generally speaking

CELIBACY and CHASTITY are expected of anyone who is unmarried in most religious traditions. Although we may live in a society where it is becoming the norm to have sexual relationships without being married, most religious traditions still believe in saving yourself for MARRIAGE.

Why do you think people believe in saving themselves for marriage? What reasons could be given for and against celibacy before you get married?

Sex before marriage can be in the form of a long-term relationship or casual sex (one-night stands) – the two are different and are viewed differently.

So why do we have sex?
The answer to that will vary – physical attraction, for love, for money, for fun, for a baby. There are probably many reasons and, at any one time, one reason may be more powerful than another. The answer will certainly influence our attitude to sex, as you will see in the religious views.

Why is adultery wrong?
ADULTERY, or having an affair, isn't illegal in Britain, but in court it counts as a valid reason for a divorce and is viewed as wrong. Adultery is usually seen as a matter of betrayal and it can destroy a relationship.

Definitions

Celibacy – not having sexual relations

Chastity – keeping oneself sexually pure

Age of consent – the age at which a person is considered old enough to have sex, according to the law

Heterosexuality – being sexually attracted to people of the opposite sex

Homosexuality – being sexually attracted to people of the same sex

Contraception – precautions taken to prevent pregnancy and protect against sexually transmitted diseases

Adultery – having sexual relations with someone other than your husband/wife

Monogamy – marriage of one man to one woman

Polygamy – marriage of one man to more than one woman at the same time

Contraception

People use CONTRACEPTION mainly to protect themselves against pregnancy. For some, there is a need to protect themselves or their partner against disease (for example, if someone is HIV positive but their partner is not, or if one of the couple is the carrier of a hereditary illness that they do not want to pass on to their future children). Attitudes to the use of contraception vary amongst the religious traditions.

There are many types of contraception – some must be supplied by doctors and others can be bought from pharmacies.

With a partner, list the types of contraception that you know of.

How do they work?

Some contraceptives block the sperm and egg so they never meet. These are barrier methods, such as the condom, cap (diaphragm) or Femidom.

Some methods ensure the woman's womb lining is altered, so that even if an egg has been fertilised, it is less likely to embed itself in the womb. The coil (IUD) works like this, as does the morning-after pill.

Some methods stop the woman from producing the egg at all, by introducing certain hormones into her system. An example of this is the Pill.

Some forms of contraception are permanent. Men and women can be sterilised so that they are no longer able to cause pregnancy or become pregnant.

Can you think of any other methods, not mentioned above?

Some people do not use artificial methods of contraception. The ones spoken about above are all artificial. Natural family planning (rhythm method) is all about the woman learning about the cycles of fertility and infertility within her own body. It relies on her knowing when she can and can't get pregnant, based on close observation of her body.

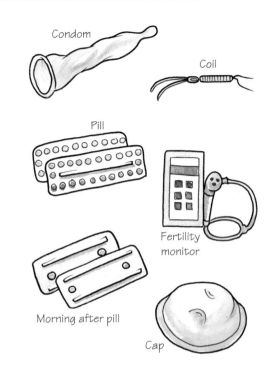

Condom

Coil

Pill

Fertility monitor

Morning after pill

Cap

The withdrawal method is perhaps the least safe method of contraception, but it is widely used. It relies on the man withdrawing from the woman before he ejaculates.

It is unlikely that you would be asked about types of contraception and how they work in the exam. However, you need to be aware of the information, so that you can understand why religions will allow their followers to use certain methods.

The Basics

① Write down what these words mean – chastity, celibacy, homosexuality, heterosexuality, contraception, adultery, age of consent.

② Why do people use contraception?

③ Why do you think most people disagree with adultery?

④ Why do you think a same sex couple might want to marry?

⑤ 'You should only have sex to have children.' Can you think of three reasons to agree with this statement and three to disagree? Write them down and explain them.

The age of consent

This is a phrase we use to talk about how old someone has to be to do something freely. In this case, we are talking about the AGE OF CONSENT for sex. It is currently sixteen for anyone in England, Wales or Scotland (seventeen in Northern Ireland). The idea is that we have to be old enough and mature enough to have sexual relationships and behave responsibly.

Many people believe that we aren't old enough or mature enough to have sex until we get married. The argument is that if you are responsible enough to have sex, you should be responsible enough to look after children. Most people in their teens wouldn't feel mature enough to look after children, even if that is what they end up doing. The religions all say you shouldn't have sex until you are married – another way of showing you aren't mature enough in your teens. Most people nowadays marry later than their teens, and the average age for marriage is going up. More and more young people stay single or unmarried until later in life.

The exam is only likely to ask you about this in a question concerning whether it is right to have different ages of consent or whether the age is too low/high. It would be an evaluative question so practise discussions about these statements:

- It's my body – no one should be able to tell me how old I must be to have sex.

- The age of consent for sex is too low at sixteen.

Don't forget to agree and disagree, and back up your argument with a few reasons. Try to explain every reason you give.

Homosexuality

HOMOSEXUALS are people who are sexually attracted to people of the same sex. Many homosexuals and lesbians (as women are called) live as couples. In 2005, they were given the right to register as couples (Civil Partnership), and so be legally recognised as a couple.

Islam condemns homosexuality and in Shariah law, there are severe punishments for those who have gay sex. Islam is in agreement with many sections of the Christian community when they say that gay sex is wrong and unnatural, because it does not lead to pregnancy and because marriage is for a man and a woman. Generally both Judaism and Sikhism agree with these reasons. Although Hinduism has no rules about homosexuality, Hindu society sees it as wrong.

All of the religions speak of tolerance and fairness, because God created all people as equals. This includes homosexuals, so they should be treated like anyone else. The problem for religious believers lies with knowing that to be true, whilst still believing that homosexuality is wrong.

A female couple at a gay pride event in London.

Check back to page 55 for a discussion on homophobia.

What the religions say

Buddhism

Ultimately, for Buddhists, sexuality has to be put aside. It is about desire and craving, which the Four Noble Truths explain we must stop if we want to achieve enlightenment.

Buddhism, in all its forms, has a very strong **celibate** tradition, with many monasteries and convents. The energy that is put into sexual activity is instead channelled into spiritual activity to try to reach enlightenment. However, there are many lay Buddhists who live as families. Sex is seen as natural, but is most rewarding as part of a loving, caring relationship, so **chastity** is encouraged. Couples should use **contraception** to limit the size of their family, and practise responsible parenthood. This can also prevent the birth of an unwanted new life that could suffer from neglect.

Buddhism encourages people to follow the Precepts, including the Precept to avoid sexual immorality such as **adultery**. Breaking that Precept will lead to suffering, causing bad karma. Karma is what determines the quality of the next life.

Buddhists do not condemn **sex before marriage** or **homosexuality**, as long as it is part of a loving, caring relationship. Where sex is based on lust, like one-night stands, it is thought of as craving that causes bad karma. In this case, it is wrong.

Christianity

Most Christians believe that only married couples should have sex together. **Chastity** is a virtue. Attitudes to the use of **contraception** vary. There is a **celibate** tradition within Christianity, such as monastic life and the priesthood.

Every sexual act must be within the framework of marriage. The Catholic Church teaches that only married couples should have sex and the most important reason for sex is to have children. There should be a chance of pregnancy within every act of sex.

Any sex other than that between husband and wife is wrong. **Sex before marriage** is fornication and therefore a sin. The same goes for masturbation, because it can't lead to pregnancy. Using contraception is against Catholic teaching because it cancels out the chance of pregnancy. Most Catholics follow natural methods of contraception, although in Western countries, this teaching is often ignored. **Homosexual** sex is thought to be unnatural and wrong because it can't lead to pregnancy.

Some Christians tolerate sex before marriage in a relationship that is leading to marriage, seeing it as an expression of love. Protestant Christians stress the need for RESPONSIBLE PARENTHOOD – only having as many children as you can properly look after. So the use of contraception is encouraged.

The BIBLE says 'Do not commit **adultery**'; Jesus says that even to look at someone lustfully is wrong, so affairs are wrong and a sin. Having an affair means you break all the promises you made before God when marrying. Christians don't agree with adultery.

Hinduism

For a Hindu man, life is split into four ashramas or stages. Sexual relationships can only happen in the second stage, when he is a married householder (grihastha). For the other three stages, the man should remain **celibate**. This means that Hindu women also only have sexual relationships within marriage. **Sex before marriage** and **homosexuality** are both against the religion. Sex is seen as a gift from the Ultimate Reality (God) and must be treated with care and respect. It is for enjoyment and to have children.

Chastity is important in Hinduism and people are expected to be virgins before marriage – their only partner should be the person they marry. Two important Hindu virtues are self-discipline and respect, and **adultery** goes against both of these values. Since adultery causes others to suffer, it brings bad karma to the adulterer and negatively affects their REINCARNATION.

Hindus do not object to using **contraception**. In fact, they encourage it. Responsible parenthood is stressed, although the need for a son rather than a daughter to carry out certain religious rituals often reduces the use of contraception. During the year, however, there are many days when couples should avoid sex – festivals, full/new moon, holy days and others adding up to 208 in total – and this obviously will act as a form of birth control.

The Basics

Look at the couples on the wall.

①

None of these couples are married. John and Sara only met last week, whereas all the others have been together for months or years. Explain what the attitude of each of your two religions would be to each couple having a sexual relationship.

②

What if Sunita and Sanjeeb got married? What would be the attitude of each religion about them having sex? What advice might be given by each religion about contraception?

Revision tip

Tips for strong answers — when asked for an attitude, the examiners want to know two things. Firstly, what the religion believes and secondly, why it believes it. If you only write down that they agree or disagree with something, you are unlikely to get more than one mark overall. You have to explain how that attitude is reached, what teachings and beliefs they have and how they link to the topics.

four

Islam

Islam does not agree with choosing never to marry nor with monastic lifestyles. It is a religious duty to marry and have children. Every person should be a virgin before marriage, and observe **chastity** before and during marriage. **Celibacy** as a life choice is wrong. The message is very clear in Islam – only married couples may have sex together. Prophet Muhammad ﷺ spoke of sex as being special within marriage. He said it was a source of pleasure and provided the blessing of children from God, if the couple so wished. This means that Muslims can and should use **contraception**. Muhammad ﷺ also said that couples should only have as many children as they could properly look after – responsible parenthood. Muslims would expect to use any appropriate form of birth control – natural or artificial. Permanent forms are frowned upon because that is a rejection of Allah's gift of children forever.

The Qur'an details specific punishments for those who have **sex before marriage**, commit **adultery** or have **homosexual** relationships. It calls these people fornicators and punishment is severe – flogging if single, execution if married. In several places, the QUR'AN specifically mentions adultery and always says it is wrong: 'Do not commit adultery. It is shameful and an evil way to act' (*Surah 17 v. 32*).

Judaism

The family is very important in Judaism. Anything that goes against this ideal is wrong. Marriage is highly recommended, whereas a life of **celibacy** is not promoted. The TORAH states that woman was made from man to be his companion. This is interpreted to mean marriage. A sex drive is healthy, and sex within marriage is for pleasure as well as for having children.

The first command given to humans was to be fruitful and multiply, understood to mean at least one boy and one girl. Various branches of Judaism have different attitudes to **contraception**. Orthodox Jews will accept it for medical/health reasons. They often use the Pill because it does not interfere in the actual act of sex and does not directly cause the wasting of seed, which is forbidden in the Torah. Reform Jews accept contraception also for social/economic reasons, and use most available methods. For all Jews, sex is forbidden at certain times within the woman's menstrual cycle. This acts as a form of birth control.

The Torah lists punishments for **sex before marriage**, **adultery** and **homosexuality**, because all are considered to be wrong. Jews are expected to be virgins before marriage, and observe **chastity** all their life. Committing adultery breaks one of the TEN COMMANDMENTS and carries the death penalty in the Torah. Jewish law calls homosexuality an abomination. Orthodox Jews maintain this view, though they state that homosexuals should not be persecuted. Many Reform and Liberal Jews accept homosexuality within loving relationships.

The family is an essential part of Jewish life.

Sikhism

Sexuality is seen as a gift from God because all beings have sexual urges. However, Sikhs warn against being controlled by your sex drive and believe it should be controlled by marriage. So **sex before marriage** is wrong and Sikhs try to protect against even the temptation of it. For example, dancing with the opposite sex is discouraged in case it leads to evil thoughts. In the Adi Granth, Sikhs are warned to avoid things that produce bad thoughts in the mind. Married life is seen as the norm – **celibacy** as a life choice isn't encouraged. **Chastity**, though, is a virtue and highly valued before and within marriage as a form of self-control. Although most Sikhs see **homosexuality** as wrong – a

form of *haumai* or selfishness – some accept it as part of what God has created in a person.

In the wedding ceremony, Sikhs make promises to be faithful. Those promises are made in front of God. The Rahit Maryada forbids **adultery** saying the touch of another man's wife is like a poisonous snake. Adultery is one of the Four Abstinences of Sikhism.

When it comes to deciding on which **contraception** to use, Sikhs can choose for themselves. They are encouraged to follow responsible parenthood – only having as many children as you can properly look after. But Sikhs would not use permanent forms of contraception, except for medical reasons, since these change the body given by God.

The Basics

①

Complete this table for each of the two religions you are studying:

Topic	Agree/disagree	Reasons why
a. Celibacy		
b. Chastity		
c. Sex before marriage		
d. Contraception		
e. Adultery		
f. Homosexuality		
g. Sex		

You will need to complete the whole row of information for each topic before moving onto the next. You don't know how much writing you'll do, so this way keeps it neat and easy to read later when you are revising.

Use these extra pages to help you to complete the table – pages 36–37, and 57–59.

②

Do you think religions should make the rules about these issues? Give some reasons and explain them.

③

Now try to argue the opposite view to the one you gave in question 2.

Now you know about attitudes to sex.

Abortion

ABORTION is the deliberate expulsion of a foetus, with the intention of destroying it.

The law in the UK (excluding Northern Ireland) says that abortion can only be carried out if two registered doctors agree that at least one of the following is true:

1   There is a danger to the woman's mental/physical health.

2   The foetus will be born with mental/physical disabilities.

3   The mental/physical health of existing children will be put at risk.

The abortion has to be carried out at a registered place, by a registered doctor before the 24th week of pregnancy.

Why some people agree with abortion ...

- It is the woman's right to decide what happens to her body.

- It can be necessary to save/protect the life of the woman.

- It would be cruel to force the woman to continue with the pregnancy.

- The foetus is only a potential life.

Why some people disagree with abortion ...

- A foetus is a potential life; and therefore abortion is murder.

- The foetus is innocent and should be protected.

- If you don't want a baby, plenty of others would love to adopt. There is no need to kill it.

- SANCTITY OF LIFE argument – that all life is sacred, including the foetus, so it must be protected.

There are many other reasons why people agree or disagree with abortion. Some people disagree because their religion tells them it is wrong. Some people agree or disagree because of their own experiences. Most people think abortion is not a good thing, but sometimes is necessary.

Research Task —

Rita knows she carries a genetic disease. She is now pregnant and the baby will probably inherit the disease and suffer greatly.

Susan became pregnant at the age of fourteen. She said she was too young to cope.

Leesa was raped and became pregnant.

Isma found out she was pregnant while she was being treated for cancer. The doctors said her treatment was vital if she was to live.

Jane was 46 when she became pregnant. The foetus was diagnosed with Downs Syndrome.

Cara became pregnant after the contraception she used failed. She is a single woman, very focused on her career.

Each of these women could ask for an abortion.

Would you agree with any? Why?

Which, if any, would you disagree with? Why?

Check the law — would they be able to get an abortion?

The Basics

① Write a definition of abortion.

② Explain what the law says about abortion.

③ Give two examples of abortion that most people would agree were necessary.

④ Write **four** reasons why some people agree with abortion.

⑤ Write **four** reasons why some people disagree with abortion.

⑥ Choose **two** of the examples of women from the box. Explain whether the law would allow them to have an abortion. Explain why you think it is right or wrong for each to have an abortion.

Buddhism and abortion

Buddhist texts do not mention abortion. Most Buddhists would not favour abortion because it is seen as killing a sentient being.

Buddhism tells us that:

- Life is special and to be protected.

- We should help others, not harm them, and reduce suffering.

- Life begins at conception.

- We should show COMPASSION (loving kindness) and practise ahimsa (non-violence).

- The main factor in the right or wrong of anything is intention.

The first and most important Precept is to refrain from taking life. Since Buddhists believe life begins at conception, abortion is killing. This would generate much bad karma for those involved, based on their intentions. Abortion does not happen by accident, so the intention breaks the Precept.

Since a person's life was decided by their karma from past lives, it may be that the suffering a life will endure is necessary for their future. By carrying out abortion, we take that chance from them.

All Buddhists should show compassion, including to the unborn, and practise ahimsa. Abortion is an act of violence and is against that value.

However, Buddhists recognise that, at times, an abortion can lead to less suffering than allowing the pregnancy to go full term, and so accept it in those circumstances.

Christianity and abortion

Many Christians believe abortion to be morally wrong. Some accept abortion in rare circumstances as a 'necessary evil'.

The Bible tells us that:

- Life is sacred.

- All humans were made in the image of God.

- God gives and takes life.

- It is wrong to kill (The Ten Commandments).

- God has planned for the life of every single one of us.

These beliefs make Christians say that abortion is usually wrong, because it means killing something sacred that God created. Only God has that right and, by allowing abortions, we take that right out of the hands of God.

The Roman Catholic Church is completely against abortion. The Didache says 'Do not kill your children by abortion'. In Vatican II, it says 'Life must be protected with the utmost care from the moment of conception'. However, if a woman needs urgent medical treatment that will also mean the death of her foetus, the Church accepts the treatment. This isn't considered to be abortion.

Protestants accept abortion as a necessary evil in some cases. Methodists and Anglicans say that it could be the 'lesser of two evils' in some circumstances. For example, many would accept it for a woman who becomes pregnant after rape or if the mother's life is at risk or if the child is likely to be born severely physically or mentally handicapped. However, they stress that great thought has to have been given and abortion has to be the absolute last resort.

Look at page 68 for questions on this topic.

four

Hinduism and abortion

Most Hindus believe abortion is wrong. However, in India, abortions are performed because Hindus wish to have a male child for religious and cultural reasons, and poverty makes it difficult to manage big families. This situation is slowly changing.

Hindu scriptures tell us that:

- Life is sacred and special, so must be respected.
- Those who carry out abortions are amongst the worst of sinners.
- All Hindus should practise ahimsa – non-violence.
- A woman who aborts her child loses her caste.
- Abortion is as bad as killing a priest or your own parents.

Obviously, abortion is wrong. Hinduism says that the foetus is a living conscious person who needs protection. The values of ahimsa and respect contradict abortion. Since we all go through many lifetimes, each creating karma for the next, when we abort a foetus we prevent that soul from working through a lifetime. This means we block that soul's progress towards union with the Ultimate Reality. It also means we make bad karma for ourselves. Some Hindu scriptures say that those who abort their children will themselves be aborted many times.

Hinduism allows abortion to save the life of the mother, as a motherless child would require more support.

Islam and abortion

Most Muslims believe abortion is wrong. Shariah (Muslim) law does allow abortion, but it is still seen as wrong.

The Qur'an and HADITH tell us that:

- Life is sacred.
- Allah has planned the life of each of us.
- We are all created individually from a clot of blood and known by Allah.
- It is wrong to kill.
- God decides the time of our birth and of our death.
- No severer of womb-relationship ties will ever enter paradise.

These beliefs make Muslims say that abortion is wrong. Abortion means killing something special that Allah has created. We destroy Allah's plans for the foetus and take away Allah's right to decide the time of our death. This is disrespectful.

Muslims dispute when the soul becomes a part of the foetus. Some say at conception; some at 48 days; some at 120 days. For some this creates a period of time when abortion may be allowed because the foetus is still just blood and cells. For others, it means abortion is wrong, other than very early abortion.

Most Muslims accept that some abortions are necessary. The most common example would be if the woman's life were at risk during the pregnancy. In this case, the woman's life would be seen as more important to save (because of her existing family and responsibilities).

Look at page 68 for questions on this topic.

four

Judaism and abortion

Most Jews would accept therapeutic abortion (for example, for medical reasons) but not simply to remove an unwanted foetus.

Jewish scriptures and law say that:

- Foetal life, like all life, is special.

- The foetus is mere water until the 40th day of pregnancy.

- We gain full human status only when we have been born.

- Abortion, under Jewish law, is not murder.

- The emphasis in Judaism is on life and new life, not destruction of life.

Judaism sees a need for abortion, but does not agree with abortion for any reason. Where a woman's life is in danger, even during childbirth, her life takes priority over the foetus and an abortion can be carried out. Some rabbis have extended the idea of endangerment to include the woman's mental health, for example, in the case of rape.

The Talmud points out that the foetus is a part of the woman, not a human in its own right. Assault on her carries a severe punishment, whereas the loss of her unborn due to that assault results in compensation only. Many rabbis now approve of abortion in cases where there is likely to be severe deformity of the foetus, for example, where the mother has had rubella.

Jews are quick to point out that abortion is not acceptable, unless for therapeutic reasons. However, exactly what counts as a therapeutic reason varies depending on Orthodox, Conservative, Liberal or Reform views.

Sikhism and abortion

Sikhism generally does not agree with abortion. It is seen as interference with God's creation.

Sikh teachings and scriptures say that:

- Life begins at conception.

- All life is special and should be respected.

- Sikhs should not harm others.

- God fills us with light so that we can be born.

- God created each of us and gave us life and it is up to God to take that life away.

For Sikhs, there is no direct teaching about abortion. Like most things, it is up to the individual to make their own decisions, guided by God. However, abortion is believed to be morally wrong because Sikhs believe life begins at conception and not at birth. In effect, abortion is seen as a form of murder since the intention is to destroy a life.

Sikhs try to live their life in worship of God, but abortion can be seen as going against God by destroying his creation. This is not worship at all.

When Sikhs become members of the Khalsa, they take vows. These include never to harm others and to do sewa (service to others). Abortion can be seen as going against both these ideals.

Look at page 68 for questions on this topic.

Protest slot

ABORTION RIGHTS (www.abortionrights.org.uk) is an organisation formed by the merger of the National Abortion Campaign and the Abortion Law Reform Association in 2003.

It campaigns for law reform and the provision of an accessible, woman-friendly, NHS-funded abortion service. It campaigns through petitions, publications and political lobbying. Much of its work is aimed at making sure the abortion laws work. For example, they try to stop doctors from blocking abortion requests.

The Basics

Answer these questions for each religion you study:

Write out the five beliefs/teachings that can be linked to abortion.

For each of the five beliefs/teachings, explain what it means for abortion. For example, if it says God gives and takes life, abortion is not God making a decision over life and so abortion would be wrong.

Explain the attitude of the religion to abortion. You must write and explain at least three ideas in your answer.

Go back to page 64, for each of the examples of women requesting an abortion, what would the religion say? What reasons might they give each time?

Now you know about attitudes to abortion.

Considering marriage

Ask most primary school children what they'll do when they grow up and they may well answer 'Get married and have a family'. Even in our society where marriage breaks down so frequently, people still have a hope of one day being married.

Why do people marry? List all the reasons that come into your mind. Compare your list with a partner's.

There must have been quite a few reasons on your joint list – emotions, needs, wishes, ability to provide, means to an end. Were any religious? Of course, religions expect their followers to marry and, of course, most of their reasons for marriage are the same as any non-religious person's. However, there are some reasons that are specifically religious. Can you think of any?

Why do religious people marry?

Perhaps the first reason is that it is a duty or expectation within their faith. Prophet MUHAMMAD ﷺ said 'Marriage is part of my example, and whoever disdains my example is not one of me' (in other words, not a Muslim). In *Genesis 2 v. 24* , Christians and Jews are told that 'a man will leave his father and mother, and be united to his wife'. For Sikhs, marriage is seen as the natural way and what God intends for all. In Hinduism, marriage is one of the stages of life. Only Buddhism has a very strong monastic code, but Buddhism still says that the householder stage (marriage) is very important as it supports those who choose a monastic life.

A second reason for marriage is to have sexual relationships and also to have children. Not all religious traditions believe that married couples must have children. They do all believe that God blesses marriage with children, though. Getting married is seen as legitimising sexual relations and keeping sex as a special act of love. Religions feel that children are more responsibly cared for within a marriage.

Why do most people feel that children should have a mum and dad who are married?

Another reason is to continue the faith. Some religions insist their followers marry people of the same tradition, such as the Sikh and Muslim faiths. It is understandable that people fear their religion will be weakened if someone marries out of the faith – why should a non-Catholic take their children to Confession and Mass, if they themselves don't believe in it? Upbringing is a very strong reason for having a faith in the first place. If you think your faith is the true way, you won't marry outside of the religion. When two people of the same faith marry, they can encourage and support each other's faith and their children will also follow it.

Finally, we must conclude that marriage provides a loving partnership within which two people can support and help each other. This overlaps with the idea of keeping the faith, but is also more about love and companionship.

A commitment being made

Christianity has marriage VOWS, which are made between a couple at a CHURCH ceremony.

What are marriage vows?

The vows are a statement of commitment. They are an agreement made between two people in the presence of many witnesses and God. Marriage is a covenant – a binding agreement or contract. When couples sign a marriage certificate, this becomes a legally binding agreement. Other religions have promises or agreements.

The vows or promises are about looking after each other through good and bad times and in sickness and in health, until death. The couple are announcing their love and commitment to this union. They are saying that they will work to keep the marriage together and support each other. That commitment brings responsibilities.

Generally in most religions, the couple share responsibility for all aspects of the marriage, although many see the man as the head of the household. Decisions should be taken together for the good of the family. Although both men and women work, the woman often takes the greater share in the upbringing of the children. Both share the role of guidance and discipline, as well as helping the faith of their children.

A Hindu couple make their promises.

In some religions, or groups within a religion, men and women have different, but equal, duties within marriage. For example, in Islam, the man deals with the outside world and provides financially for the family. He takes on the religious education of his sons when they are old enough to go to the mosque. The woman has responsibility for the home and for looking after the children. The Qur'an says that a man and his wife are like garments for each other. In other words, they should comfort, help and support each other. This idea is common to all religions.

A Christian couple exchange wedding rings.

The Basics

① Why do religious people marry?

② How is marriage a covenant?

③ What are the marriage responsibilities for religious couples?

Research Task —

Find out what the marriage promises or vows are for each of the two religions you are studying.

Marriage ceremonies

Buddhist wedding

Buddhism does not have a set ceremony for marriage. In fact, Buddhist monks are forbidden from attending any ceremonies, because they have renounced worldly life. So the ceremonies are completely non-religious.

A couple will choose a lucky day for their wedding. Often, they will have visited a monk to have their fortunes read and the date is decided from that reading.

June						
Mon	Tue	Wed	Thur	Fri	Sat	Sun
				1	2	3
4	(5)	6	7	8	9	10
11	12	13	14	15	16	17
18	19	20	21	22	23	24
25	26	27	28	29	30	

In each country, Buddhists will follow the local customs for marriage, which may include registering their marriage officially.

Later, the couple might visit the monastery or temple, or invite a monk to come to bless their marriage, by reciting verses from Buddhist scriptures. He might also answer any questions they have about being married Buddhists.

The couple might then invite the monk to a feast as a sign of their thanks for his blessing.

tasks

① For each of the two religions you are studying, write about the marriage ceremony. One religion is featured on each of the next few pages. It is described briefly and pictures are given of the most important points. You need to write about them all if you want to get full marks in the exam.

② Your description of the marriage could include drawings and writing.

③ If you know more details about any ceremony, then include those too. This might include the symbolism of any element of the ceremony.

Christian wedding

Marriage is a sacrament in some Christian traditions – it brings a blessing from God. Let's look at the Roman Catholic ceremony where marriage takes place as part of the Mass.

The couple will come to church to be united in marriage by the priest. He greets them before the whole congregation.

The priest then reads a *homily* – a speech about marriage and what it means in the Christian context.

The priest asks three set questions to the bride and groom to make sure they understand the responsibilities of marriage.

The couple make their vows to each other.

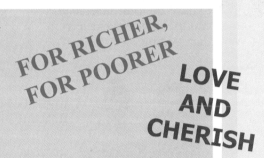

FOR RICHER, FOR POORER

LOVE AND CHERISH

The priest declares they have agreed to marry before God and accepts their decision. At this point he says 'What God has joined together, let no man put asunder.'.

The rings are blessed and exchanged.

The priest blesses the marriage.

The couple sign the marriage register. This is the civil bit of the ceremony.

Research Task –

Find more details and pictures to illustrate your description of the marriage ceremonies. The BBC website, www.bbc.co.uk, has a great religion section with lots of facts and pictures of all the ceremonies. It gives you links to other websites with information and pictures of the ceremonies. It also has lots of information about attitudes to marriage.

Hindu wedding

Find out all about Hindu marriage on the website www.vivaaha.org. The wedding ceremony is part of a whole set of ceremonies that lead up to and follow the ceremony itself. We will concentrate on the actual ceremony.

The groom, his family and friends arrive for the wedding to be received by the bride's family.

Under a specially-built canopy, the priest begins the ceremony with a blessing on the couple. The bride and groom give each other garlands.

The father pours out sacred water to show that he gives away his daughter, whilst the priest recites hymns from the Vedas. The groom also accepts his duties and responsibilities as a husband.

The bride and groom face each other. The end of her scarf is tied to his shirt to symbolise their eternal union. They exchange their rings.

Holding hands, the couple throw samagree – a mixture of sandalwood, herbs, sugar, rice and ghee – into the sacred fire. The bride also offers rice. These are to ask for the deities' blessing on their marriage.

The bride and groom walk three times round the fire, reciting hymns and prayers.

At the end of each circuit of the fire, they both step onto a stone to pray that their marriage will be strong like the stone.

They then take seven steps round the fire and with each one make a wedding promise.

The ceremony ends with a prayer that the marriage cannot be broken.

Muslim wedding

Traditionally, Muslim marriages last up to five days because of the many cultural traditions (depending upon which Muslim country or area is involved). We will concentrate on the actual wedding ceremony itself.

The ceremony, which takes place on day four of a five-day celebration, is called NIKKAH. It is always a simple ceremony and is performed by an imam. Most nikkah are performed at the home of the bride or groom and not the mosque.

The groom has to declare a mahr – a dowry, showing his respect for her. It can include anything she has asked for – money, clothes or even a house. The groom can pay this over time and the bride keeps the dowry, whatever happens.

An IMAM usually leads the ceremony, but it could be any respected male. Often, the bride does not attend the ceremony herself and is represented by someone else, usually her father. She will already have given her consent beforehand.

Vows are not compulsory, but some couples do make them. They will usually have written marriage contracts beforehand about what they expect from the marriage and what each other's rights will be once they are married.

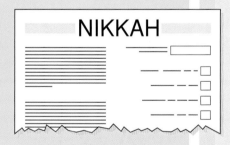

The imam announces their intention to marry and asks if anyone has any objections. He also recites some verses from the Qur'an and the Nikkah Khutba, which talk about the purpose of marriage.

The consent of the bride is asked for three times by the imam. After it is given, the marriage is complete.

four

Jewish wedding

Jewish weddings begin with the signing of the KETUBAH or marriage contract. It details the legal terms of the marriage. It is often a very ornate and beautiful work – more like art than a contract. This is done before four witnesses.

The bridegroom places a veil over the bride's face, to show that he will protect and look after his wife.

The bride and groom go to the huppah (wedding canopy), where the bride walks around the groom up to seven times.

The couple drink a glass of wine – the first of seven to represent the seven days of creation and the start of the building of a marriage.

The ring is given to the bride or rings are exchanged. It isn't compulsory for the man to have a ring. It must be a plain, unbroken circle, with no decoration, to emphasise the hope for a harmonious marriage.

The RABBI will make a speech about the responsibilities of marriage and about the couple. Prayers will be said. The cantor will sing.

The ceremony ends when the groom crushes a glass under his foot. This remembers the destruction of the temple, but also shows the hope that bad luck will not come to the marriage. There is a tradition that a wicked spirit visits each wedding to see what trouble it can cause. Breaking the glass gives it the trouble it came for. With this act, the marriage is complete.

four

Sikh wedding

Look at the website www.sikhs.org/wedding for more detail and pictures. Sikh marriage is called Anand Karaj. Only Sikhs can have this ceremony. Anyone who is a full KHALSA SIKH can lead the ceremony.

The groom listens to kirtan songs in the GURDWARA as he waits for his bride to arrive. When she arrives, she sits on his left in front of the GURU GRANTH SAHIB. The Ardas prayer will be said to begin the ceremony. This prayer begins and ends all ceremonies.

The end of the scarf is placed in the hands of the bride, while four lavan (verses of a hymn written by the fourth Guru) from the Guru Granth Sahib are read.

When the second lavan is reached, the couple stand and the groom leads them slowly around the Guru Granth Sahib. They do this for each lavan.

The ragis read out the Anand Sahib and a randomly chosen hymn from the Guru Granth Sahib is read out.

The ceremony ends with the Ardas prayer, and the distribution of karah parshad (blessed food) to all.

> ## Revision tip
>
> Although it is good to research as much information as possible, you will never need to say that much in the exam. Make sure you know the **main points** and can say them in the right order. Writing the important points, with a little explanation, is usually enough to get you full marks.

Now you know about marriage ceremonies.

four

Talking children

When a couple marry, at some point they usually think about having children. Most religious people will have children within their marriage.

Why do you think people decide to have children?

For most religions having children is part of their religious duty. God told Jews and Christians to go forth and multiply – in other words, to have children. Most religions see children as a gift from God, a blessing on the marriage.

How do religious people bring up their children?

Most people want the same or better chances for their children than they had themselves.
If they are religious, they believe in their faith as the true way to heaven, paradise, enlightenment or nirvana. They want their children to have the best possible lives and afterlives, so they want their children to follow their religion:

- They will teach the children how to **live their faith**.

- They will teach them **how to behave** – according to that religion.

- They will make sure they are made **members of that religion** through **special ceremonies**.

- They will make sure they learn **how to worship**.

Do you think it is difficult in Britain today to follow a religion? With a partner, discuss what makes it easy and what makes it hard.

British society is very secular. This means our society does not live by fixed religious laws or behaviours and religion is not the main focus of British culture. Most people don't even practise a religion in any way. For many religious people, their home is a spiritual place and they go to a religious building to carry out an act of worship with others. In a way, this means they have two different worlds to live in, which can make life difficult. Religious parents still try to bring their children up in their faith and make them understand how to keep that faith in a secular country.

The Basics

①
Write three reasons why couples choose to have children.

②
How do religious people bring up their children?

③
Explain why it can be difficult for a religious couple to bring up a child in a non-religious society.

four

Birth and initiation ceremonies

Buddhism

There are no set religious practices for Buddhists. Any ceremonies held comes from the culture of the country in which they are held, rather than from the religion.

Some families, especially in Theravada Buddhist cultures, want a monk to bless their child. The monk will visit the home and chant some religious texts as a blessing. To show their thanks, the couple will give gifts of food, money or other things to the monk and to his monastery.

Christianity

Christians have infant baptism and dedication ceremonies. If you are asked about an initiation ceremony in the exam, you could talk about either. This section looks at the infant baptism service because this is more complex. This ceremony differs between Christian denominations.

The parents bring their child to the church for baptism. Baptism welcomes the baby into the faith and the child becomes a member of the religion. For Catholics it also means the baby is washed clean of sins inherited from its ancestors.

The baby is usually dressed in white, for purity. Everyone gathers around the font for the ceremony.

Hinduism

In Hinduism, there are two very early BIRTH/INITIATION CEREMONIES. Hindus in different parts of India will also have cultural ceremonies. There are a number of other ceremonies as well, a little later in the child's life.

The first ceremony is called Jatakarma and happens as soon after birth as possible. At this time, the father will put a little ghee (butter) mixed with honey onto the baby's tongue. This is in the hope that the baby will have a good nature. The father will also whisper the name of the Ultimate Reality into the baby's ear, so that the baby is welcomed into the faith.

The second ceremony usually happens on the tenth to twelfth day after birth. It is called Namakarana and is the name-giving ceremony. The baby is dressed in new clothes and can be taken to the temple, or a BRAHMIN PRIEST will come to the home.

Many Buddhists take their child to the temple soon after it is born. They want to give thanks to the BUDDHA for their child, so they pray and make offerings of incense, flowers, food and money to show their gratitude.

They may want the child to receive its name at the TEMPLE. Often in such ceremonies, water is sprinkled over the child. Water symbolises cleanliness and protection from evil. Again the parents will make offerings as gifts to the Buddha and the temple.

The priest asks the parents and godparents some questions about their faith, and their intention to bring the baby up in the faith. He takes some water from the font and makes the sign of the CROSS on the baby's forehead. The cross is the symbol for Christianity, of course.

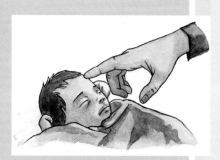

Water is poured over the baby's forehead three times – representing God the Father, God the Son and God the Holy Spirit.

In many churches, the family will be given a lighted candle to represent Jesus as the Light of the World. It will be a reminder of their promises to bring the child up in the faith.

An astrologer will read out the child's horoscope, which he has prepared after the child was born, and the name is announced.

Those present sing songs and hymns to show happiness and thanksgiving. Many families will make a fire sacrifice (havan). They offer grain and ghee to the deities through the flames of a fire, whilst chanting mantras.

tasks

1. Read through the account of the initiation ceremony for each of the two religions you are studying.

2. Make notes of the important elements.

3. Draw a cartoon strip to show the elements of each ceremony.

4. Label the symbolism involved in each service.

four

Islam

There are two main ceremonies – the Tahneek and the Aqiqah.

The Tahneek ceremony happens as soon as possible after birth. The father whispers the Adhan into each ear, right then left. The child hears the call to prayer and the name of Allah, and so the child is welcomed into the faith.

The father then takes the child and places the soft part of a date on its tongue. This shows the hope for the child to be sweet-natured when he or she gets older.

The Aqiqah ceremony is the naming ceremony. It takes place a few days after birth. The parents shave the baby's head and weigh the hair. The family will give at least its equivalent weight in money to charity. This purifies the child.

Judaism

Boys and girls have different birth ceremonies in Judaism. A boy should be circumcised eight days after birth, as a reminder of the covenant between Abraham and the Israelites.

A mohel (person trained to carry out circumcision) goes to the home of the child. A special guest (sandek) will hold the child while the circumcision is carried out. They are known as a special guest because this role is considered an honour. The person may be a friend of the family or a relative.

The father will read a blessing from the Torah. Then the mohel blesses the child and announces its name.

Sikhism

As soon as possible after birth, the father whispers the Mool Mantra into the ear of the child. This means it has been welcomed into the faith. He also puts a little honey onto the baby's lips, in the hope of giving the child a sweet future.

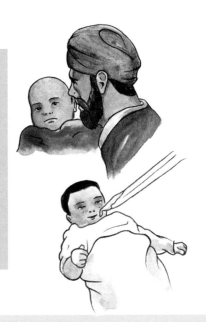

The naming ceremony takes place at the first gurdwara service after birth if possible. The couple take their child to the service, along with the ingredients for karah parshad and a romalla (an embroidered cloth to cover the Guru Granth Sahib) as a gift for the gurdwara.

There are readings of thanksgiving from the Guru Granth Sahib. The granthi stirs the amrit (holy water) with a kirpan (sword) and then drops some into the mouth of the baby. The granthi also says a prayer for long life and sweetness for the baby.

Verses from the Qur'an are read aloud and the child's name is announced. Again, the father will whisper the Adhan into the baby's ear.

The family will pay for an animal to be sacrificed and its meat is given to the poor to give thanks for the gift of a child.

Finally everyone joins in a feast to celebrate the birth of the child.

The baby is then given to the mother to be fed.

The family and their guests celebrate with a party.

A girl is announced and named on the first Sabbath after her birth. This happens at the synagogue. Many Jews follow the zeved habit ceremony where, on the seventh day after birth, a rabbi comes to bless the baby girl and the family enjoy a meal of celebration.

At the next stage, the name is chosen. The granthi opens the Guru Granth Sahib at random and reads the first word on the left-hand page. The parents use the first letter of this word for the first letter of the baby's name. The granthi then announces that name to the congregation.

The karah parshad is given out to everyone in the service. This is considered to be blessed food from God.

The couple arrange a donation that will go to the poor, as a sign of their thanks to God for their child.

Now you know about initiation ceremonies.

Divorce and remarriage

DIVORCE is the legal dissolution of a marriage. Current figures suggest that more than one in three first marriages end in divorce in the UK.

Why do marriages fail? Are there any reasons you find more, or less, acceptable?

When divorce looms

Religious traditions view marriage as a very special, even sacred act. None of them wish to see marriages end and so they encourage the couple to work at their marriage. The initial commitment made, with its related responsibilities, is not to be taken lightly.

What options are there generally in society to help when marriages meet difficulties?

Apart from the efforts the couple might make to sort out their problems, the family will be an important source of support and guidance. In religious traditions where arranged marriage is practised, the family is very important. The Qur'an states that if a marriage is in danger 'send for an arbiter from his family and (one) from her family'. Arbiters use counselling and arbitration to try to solve the problems and help the marriage to get back on track. It is hoped that the marriage will be saved by the counselling.

Other friends or acquaintances who attend the same place of worship may also try to counsel a couple. Christians try to help other couples with advice and prayers for God's guidance and support.

The religious leader – for example, the priest or VICAR – can give the couple advice and listen to them. They will mediate and counsel them to try to see a way forward.

The couple may even be encouraged to temporarily separate.

How might each of these ways of helping a couple prove helpful?

Most religious people accept divorce as a last resort, after everything else has failed. Buddhists, for example, believe that sometimes divorce causes less suffering than staying together. Compassion and relief of suffering are important to Buddhists. Most Christians believe divorce has to be an option, even if they don't think it right to marry again afterwards.

Revision tip

The exam often asks about how religious people can help couples who are having difficulties in their marriage. The answer is the same as for any non-religious person. Of course, religious people will also pray for them and with them, give them religious advice and use the Bible to comfort and guide them. Make sure your answer has a religious start, but you can include all the non-religious ways too.

Religious attitudes to divorce and remarriage

Buddhism

There isn't a religious contract for marriage, so divorce doesn't carry strict religious attitudes. REMARRIAGE is acceptable.

Buddhism teaches:

- We should keep the Five Precepts.

- We should cultivate compassion within ourselves.

- All our words, thoughts and deeds create good and bad karma for our future rebirths.

- We should practise ahimsa (non-violence) in every form.

This all means that, for Buddhists, divorce is sometimes the best option. Two people should not make each other's lives more difficult by staying together. By not divorcing, they cause suffering to each other, which goes against the ideas of compassion and ahimsa. They may break the Precepts if they hurt each other emotionally and use language unkindly. By breaking those Precepts, they create bad karma for themselves, which has to be worked through in a later rebirth.

This doesn't mean that Buddhists say everyone should simply divorce at the first sign of trouble. Marriage carries great responsibilities and divorce is a major decision, not to be taken lightly. Buddhism emphasises that, in these circumstances, sensitivity and support are the most important qualities.

Christianity

The Roman Catholic Church forbids divorce, but allows ANNULMENT. Most other Christian groups allow divorce as a last resort. The Christian attitude to remarriage varies from person to person.

Christianity teaches:

- 'God hates divorce' – Old Testament.

- Couples should stay together 'until death us do part' (wedding vows).

- A man who divorces his wife makes her an adulterer. Adultery carried the death sentence in Jesus' time.

- Marriage is a sacrament, so sacred.

- Forgiveness and love, according to Jesus' preachings.

The intention of the wedding vows is that divorce will not take place. A couple promise to stay together until death, not to let anyone come between them and to honour each other.

As marriage is a SACRAMENT, with God blessing the couple, Roman Catholics will not allow divorce.

Marriages can be annulled as a declaration that the marriage bond did not exist. For example, if one of them cannot fulfil their marital duties.

Other Christian groups, such as Methodists, allow divorce. They see it as a legitimate last option when all ways to resolve problems have been exhausted. Jesus taught forgiveness and giving a second chance, so it would be an act of Christian love to allow divorce for some couples. Many Christians also recognise that couples can't always be blamed for divorce, so the pair should not be prevented from finding love in another marriage.

Answer the questions on page 85 about this topic.

Religious attitudes to divorce and remarriage

Hinduism

The highest caste of Hindus – Brahmin – is forbidden divorce according to Hindu law. Divorce does happen at all levels but it is not very common because of the social stigma attached to it.

Hinduism teaches:

- Marriage is a lifelong union.

- Marriage is a sacred COVENANT.

- 'I promise never to abandon her, whatever happens' – a wedding promise.

- Marriage is part of the spiritual journey through life.

- Divorce is forbidden to Brahmins, according to scripture.

Marriage is seen as part of the spiritual journey of all people. Any problems should be dealt with and worked through together. Giving up on a marriage is thought of as failing in the spiritual journey, which creates bad karma for your future reincarnation.

Although Hindu scriptures don't forbid divorce to most Hindus, in reality, divorce is rare. Marriage is seen as a key institution that keeps society in order. As a result, society views divorce as a shameful thing and so people are less willing to divorce.

The Hindu Marriage Act of 1955 in India allowed divorce on certain grounds. These include obvious things like cruelty or adultery, but also things like converting to a different religion or having certain diseases.

Islam

Islamic law allows divorce to all people.

Islam teaches:

- Marriage is part of the Sunnah (custom).

- The lawful thing Allah hates most is divorce, according to the HADITH.

- A woman may obtain a divorce.

- 'Marry and do not divorce; the throne of Allah shakes due to divorce' (Hadith)

- 'If you fear a breach between a man and his wife, appoint two arbiters' (Qur'an)

Islam accepts the need for divorce, but insists that couples try to resolve their differences first. Shariah Law states that a Muslim couple must use mediators before they seek divorce.

The divorce is quite straightforward. The man states 'I divorce you' three times, in front of four reliable witnesses. There is then a waiting period of three months, to make sure the woman is not pregnant. During this time, the couple must not have sex, he must not throw her out and he must continue to maintain her lifestyle. At the end of the three months, he has to pay the remaining dowry to her. This is one reason why dowries now contain items such as a house or a car, as it ensures the woman is financially stable after a divorce. If the woman is pregnant, the divorce is postponed until the baby does not need to be fed by its mother.

A woman can seek a divorce called Khul. If she does this then she has to repay her own dowry. Few women can afford these repayments so such a divorce is rare. In our changing society, it may become more common.

Remarriage is not a problem, although divorced people find it more difficult to meet a partner because Muslim society does not really approve of divorce.

Answer the questions on page 85 about this topic.

Judaism

Judaism allows divorce, but only as a last resort because marriage is special and sacred.

Judaism teaches:

- Marriage is a sacred act.

- 'When a man puts aside the wife of his youth, even the very altar weeps' (Talmud).

- 'God hates divorce' (Neviim).

- Divorce is acceptable through a bill of divorce (Torah).

- 'A court can grant a woman divorce, if she can show that she can no longer live with him' (Maimonides).

Since marriage is sacred, with God as a witness, divorce is not viewed well. This reduces the number of divorces in more Orthodox groups of Jews. The actual process includes a period of delay time, which gives a chance for reconciliation.

A husband serves a bill of divorce, known as a *get*, to his wife before three judges of the Beth Din (Jewish court of law) and witnesses. None of the people may be related to either husband or wife, or each other.

The actual get has to be written in a specific way in front of the judges – black ink, Hebrew square-character style, no mistakes and on unblemished parchment. It is prohibited to issue a get on Shabbat or holy days.

Remarriage is not a problem. However, a woman may not marry for at least three months after divorce. This is to make sure she is not pregnant, so that the paternity of any child is clear.

Sikhism

Divorce is not the Sikh way, but civil divorces are accepted by the faith. Marriage is seen as a lifetime commitment that should not be broken. Sikh virtues such as tolerance and patience should strengthen marriage.

Sikhism teaches:

- Married life is the normal state for all people.

- Marriage is a sacrament.

- Marriage is a permanent relationship, and divorce is not allowed for, according to the Anand Marriage Act of 1909.

- In the marriage ceremony, a lifelong commitment is made.

- Marriage is considered to be two souls in one body.

Sikhism does not favour divorce and families will do all they can to help a couple to solve their problems. However, Sikhs always live by the laws of the land in which they reside. This means that if divorce is permitted under British law then Sikhs can have access to it. As with most things, this is a matter for each individual's conscience and not for public debate. If a Sikh couple, having tried to solve their problems, still wish to divorce then it is allowed.

Remarriage is not a problem. Since Sikhs believe marriage to be the most natural state of all, remarriage is encouraged. The marriage would again take place in the gurdwara before the Guru Granth Sahib.

task

① Explain the attitude of the two religions you have studied to divorce. Include teachings in your answer.

Now you know about divorce and remarriage.

four

Exam Tips

Technical language

These are the words specific to the subject or topic. This unit has lots of technical language and you have to know all of it. Start by learning the important words in the unit and put them all into your glossary. These words are: **denomination, abortion, sanctity of life, covenant, celibacy, chastity, adultery, arranged marriage** and **divorce**.

Why is it so important to learn all these words? You might be asked to explain what any one of them means. If you don't know, you can't get the marks. Also, suppose the question was 'Explain religious attitudes to abortion' for eight marks and you didn't understand 'abortion'. Learn those words – it is the start of the revision journey and the path to a good grade.

The exam may also ask about the ceremonies from this unit. There are two – the **marriage ceremony** and the **initiation (birth) ceremonies**.

You need to know the important points of each ceremony. Just stating those points in order will give you most, if not all, of the marks available. To make sure you get all the marks, include some explanation of any symbolic part of the ceremony.

Let's see if you can answer these questions that use technical terms.

1 Explain what is meant by 'sanctity of life' and show how it applies to the issue of abortion. (4 marks)

2 What responsibilities do husbands and wives take on in the two religions you have studied? (6 marks)

3 Describe an initiation ceremony in each of the two religions you have studied. (8 marks)

4 Besides bringing up children, explain two other purposes of marriage according to a religious tradition. (4 marks)

5 Explain attitudes towards divorce and remarriage in two religious traditions you have studied. (8 marks)

6 State three reasons why religious people would regard adultery as wrong. (3 marks)

Did you find any of those questions difficult? Try these tips to help you gain maximum marks on each.

1 First, say what it means. Next, say what a person who believes in this would think of abortion – is it right or wrong?

2 Use any vows or promises to help you – go through them because they are telling you what responsibilities a couple take on. Explaining what each will mean in terms of married life will push you into the higher level of the available marks.

3 State the important points, in order, and explain the symbolism of at least one of the points.

4 Ignore the first half; just explain two purposes of marriage.

5 You must give the attitudes of the two religions separately – as if you have been asked the same question twice. It makes your answer clearer and better. Generally, if a religion allows divorce, it also allows remarriage.

6 Of course, choose religious reasons as far as possible. Use everyday responses only when you run out of religious ones.

four

Exam Tips

Command words

These are the words the exam boards use to describe instructions. Make sure you answer questions in the way they need to be answered. It is easy to respond in the wrong way and lose marks.

The most common command words/phrases are –

- **State** – list briefly

- **Explain** – give detail about any point you make

- **Describe** – write a description, in order

- **More than one point of view** – agree and disagree

Look at some examples of questions containing each of these words/phrases and try to answer them. You will notice that 'state' questions are usually only worth one or two marks, whereas 'explain' questions are worth more. Use the number of marks available to help you decide how much detail to include. If it is worth four marks, so be sure to explain and give examples.

1 State two reasons why women might decide to have abortions. (2 marks)

2 State some reasons why religious people might disagree with divorce. (2 marks)

3 Explain the roles of men and women in marriage. (4 marks)

4 Explain attitudes to sex in each of the two religions you have studied. (8 marks)

5 Explain why religious people might not agree with abortion. (4 marks)

6 Describe a wedding ceremony in each of the two religions you have studied. (10 marks)

7 'Same sex couples should not be allowed to marry.' Do you agree? Give reasons and explain your answer, showing you have thought about more than one point of view. Refer to religious arguments in your answer. (5 marks)

5 Animals and the Environment

Does the world belong to humans? Can we use it in whichever way we choose?

The answers to these questions depend upon a person's own view of the natural world and how we treat it, but the answers can also be influenced by religious thinking.

This unit is based on several concepts. The first one is SANCTITY OF LIFE. This is the idea that life was created by God, and is special and unique by its very existence. The whole of nature can be considered life – when we talk about life as sacred, do we need to include the natural world? What about animals? If their lives are sacred, the implications are massive.

Next, we have the concept of STEWARDSHIP or, in this case, the role of looking after the world and everything natural. If humans have this role, what can we say about how well we are performing this task?

While studying the issues, you need to consider the following points:

Does the world belong to us?

Do we have a duty or role to take care of the world?

Does all life, including animals and nature, deserve respect?

Dog fighters imprisoned

More medicine finds in shrinking rainforest

Big increase in environmentally-friendly holidays

Research Task —

Go through the newspapers for the next two weeks. Keep a record of all the stories involving humans and nature. Look at the overall picture — how are we treating the natural world? Are we using it as we wish or are we taking measures to protect it? What measures are being taken? Why should we do things to look after it?

The issues

This unit deals with a huge range of issues. The examination can ask you about any of them so you need to know about all of the different issues, so you are ready for the one or more that may come up. The religious attitudes are similar each time because they are based on just a few principles.

Pollution

There are many types of pollution. Generally, we talk about water, land and air pollution. Pollution is something that is dumped or released – it might be a dangerous substance or one that is not hazardous until there is too much of it. It could be something emptied into water that kills the fish or makes it undrinkable; rubbish that makes areas untidy and unsafe; or exhaust fumes from cars affecting people's breathing.

Example – at Bhopal, in India, a leak from a chemical factory poisoned an entire town. Thousands of people died and people are still suffering today, over twenty years later.

Global warming

Scientists tell us that the world is getting warmer. This change will lead to the ice caps melting, causing the seas to rise and land to be lost under the sea. Global warming will affect crop production, as well as reducing the land space where humans live. Many of the very poorest areas of the world will be greatly affected too. Pollution is thought to contribute to global warming.

Example – much of the Netherlands lies on land reclaimed from the sea and the south-east of England is very low-lying. Reclaimed and low-lying land would be lost with dramatic rises in sea level.

Consumption of natural resources

Natural resources include vegetation, minerals and fossil fuels. Humans are using these in greater quantities and at a faster rate now than at any other time in our history. Some resources, such as fossil fuels, are running out. Fossil fuels are limited in quantity and take millions of years to be formed. We either have to stop using them or find a different source of energy that is renewable.

Example – oil may run out this century.

Deforestation

This is the destruction of huge areas of forest, usually to create grazing land for cattle or to create areas for building, mining or roads. The planet needs trees to convert the carbon dioxide we breathe out into the oxygen we breathe in. The rainforests also contain many plants that can be used as medicines, and these are lost with deforestation. There are also thought to be many species of animals and plants that we haven't even recorded yet in the rainforests – they could become extinct before we have even discovered them.

Example – an area the size of Wales is cut down from the Amazon rainforest every year for cattle grazing.

Destruction of natural habitats

This is partly due to deforestation, but is also a result of land clearance for building factories, farming and for people to live. When we clear the vegetation, we take away the homes of some animals. We also destroy plants, sometimes putting the species in danger of extinction. Some of these plants could have become valuable medicines.

Example – clearing green areas in the UK to build new houses.

Genetic modification of animals, plants and crops

This is when scientists take the DNA from one living thing (everything that grows has DNA) and then modify it, sometimes by adding DNA from another living thing. By doing this, they create a new strain or species that has a different strength, or ability, or has a weakness removed.

Example – scientists have created new types of rice that grow faster, allowing more than one harvest per year. This means that in certain climatic conditions, more food can be grown.

The Basics

For each of the topics on pages 89–91, answer these questions:

①

Explain what it is and give an example of it.

②

Explain why it causes concern.

③

Explain whether it shows respect for the world.

④

'Humans are more important than the environment and animals.' Do you agree with this statement? Give reasons and explain your answer. Argue from two different points of view. Use some religious arguments in your answer.

Factory farming

Farms are necessary to meet consumer demands for food, but factory farming is a controversial issue. Its main aim is to increase the production levels of meat, eggs, milk and other produce rather than to look after the animals. Factory farming maximises the space it uses and therefore animals are mainly kept in sheds. The process of farming is highly industrialised and mechanised.

Example – hens in battery farms live their lives in small cages where they cannot move around. Their beaks are clipped to prevent them hurting themselves or others and when they stop producing enough eggs, they are killed.

Animals are sometimes killed for their fur, which is then used in the fashion industry. To meet the demand for fur, wild animals are put into farms. They are unnaturally caged throughout their lives, often in the wrong climate. For example, silver foxes from Siberia are farmed in Korea.

Experimentation

Millions of animals are bred for use in experimentation every year. These are mainly live animal experiments.

Experimentation may be used to test:

- The effectiveness of a new medicine (i.e. how well it works and what the side effects are).

- The toxicity of a new product (i.e. how much of it can be consumed before it kills or maims).

- The excessive use or lack of use of something (for example, how we are affected by not sleeping).

There are many groups opposed to the use of experimentation. They claim it is cruel (for example, in the Draize test, liquid is continually dripped into a rabbit's eye to see the whole range of its effects), unnecessary (tissue cultures from humans can now be used for testing) and also ineffective (humans are different from animals and so results from the tests can never be guaranteed).

Hunting

Hunting came from a need to find food and clothing. Fur and animal skin were recognised as good materials in the cold before synthetic materials were invented. Hunting is also a sport. Many people think hunting for food is acceptable, as the animal is usually caught and killed with minimum suffering. However, many people consider hunting for fur or for sport to be unacceptable. Hunting for sport relies on a catch that takes the time, skill and guile of the hunter – a quick catch and kill is no challenge. Many feel this leads to unnecessary levels of suffering for the animal. There is also the problem that some animals have been hunted to near extinction. Even though there are strict laws in the UK, some activities, such as poaching, are still a problem. Example – fox hunting has been banned in the UK.

Zoos

These are places to visit where we keep animals for our pleasure and interest. Originally, it meant that you could see unusual animals that you wouldn't normally be able to see.

The animals are kept in cages and enclosures, and so don't have the space, conditions or climate they would have naturally. Some zoos, especially in poorer or developing countries, make animals live in very cruel conditions.

However, zoos also play a big part in breeding rare animals and have contributed to preventing the extinction of some species. Many animals that have disappeared from the wild are bred in zoos. In these cases, the zoos represent the species' only hope for survival.
Example – the London Zoo has bred many rare species.

tasks

Try evaluating these statements:

① Everybody has to look after the world and animals if we want to save them.

② There is no good excuse for using animals as slaves.

Now you know the issues concerning animals and the environment.

Whose world is it?

Newsflash. Today, the local council has agreed to allow a bypass road to be built around the town cutting through approximately 600 acres of previously protected greenbelt and farmland. Habitats of endangered species will be relocated. The Great Green Children's Park will be lost, but it may be built somewhere else in the future. The introduction of the road will mean heavy traffic will go around, not through, the town. As a result, the air will be cleaner and healthier for all, particularly helping the old and young of the town. There should be a reduction in the number of illnesses linked to breathing problems.

Town centre shopping will benefit as parts of the old road will be turned into pedestrian-only sections. Some new housing will be built to help ease current housing shortages. A few very old streets will be demolished.

Plans to redevelop the old factory area have now been dropped – the money is being used for the road scheme.

tasks

Read the newsflash.

① Read the list below of the effects of the new road. Split them into advantages and disadvantages. For each of the effects, explain what makes it an advantage or disadvantage. Be aware that some could be both. The effects:

Destroying habitats of endangered species.
Cleaner air in town.
Loss of children's play park.
Factory complex to be left as it is.

Greenbelt land lost.
Pedestrian zones created.
New housing created.
Old housing destroyed.

② The people below will all be affected by the new scheme. Do you think they'd agree with the scheme? Explain why.

a. Bill (farmer) – I'm old and my kids don't want to work the farm. I've been offered a lot of money by the Council to sell up.
b. Suzi (mum of two small children) – Sam and Sara love that park. There isn't really anywhere else to play. The town will be cleaner and safer for them, though.
c. Dave (environmentalist) – these animals and insects will all die if their relocation isn't done by experts. If not done properly, it will be a disaster.
d. Chris (construction company worker) – sounds like a lot of work will come my firm's way out of this. It will stop my weekend country walk though.

This is a complicated issue. It isn't just a case of looking after people or looking after nature (stewardship). Often making progress in one area has an impact on other areas, and we have to try to sort the other problems out as a result.

The religions recognise the tension between looking after people and looking after the environment. However, they say we must do both, because all life is sacred and humans depend on the environment.

What about food?

Would you eat dog, snake, insects or brains, if you were offered them?

Do you have any rules about what foods you will eat?

Some people will try any food they are offered. Some people will only eat food that they recognise from their own culture. Some people eat no meat (VEGETARIAN), while some eat neither meat nor dairy products (vegan). Some people follow strict food rules because of their job (like sportsmen) or their religion.

Why do people have rules about food?

It may be how they were brought up. If no one around you ever eats grilled newborn mice, you probably won't think it sounds too appetising! In some Asian countries, they'd disagree.

It could be that your religion tells you that some foods cannot be eaten together or eaten at all. For example, Jewish people do not eat meat and milk products together because of laws in the TORAH. In some cases your health stops you eating certain things. If you are allergic to nuts, you must avoid them to stay alive. Perhaps you feel it is wrong to eat certain foods. You might think it is wrong to eat meat because of how animals are treated on farms.

Christianity has no special food rules, but would expect there to be no cruelty involved in the production of meat. Some Western Christians do not eat meat on Fridays to remember Jesus died on that day.

Buddhism, **Hinduism** and **Sikhism** are essentially vegetarian in practice. For Buddhists and Hindus, this reflects their belief in ahimsa and compassion, as well as their respect for all life. KHALSA vows forbid Sikhs to eat meat that has been killed ritually.

Islam forbids the eating of pork, as the pig is thought to be an unclean animal. The QUR'AN forbids the eating of any animal not ritually killed and of animals of prey. Muslims must always follow halal – that which is lawful – and that includes the food they eat.

Judaism has the most detailed food rules (kashrut). Meat and milk may not be eaten together. Certain animals – pig, animals without cloven hoof, birds of prey and fish without fins, scales and backbone – are forbidden. Any meat must be cleaned of its blood and must be from an animal that was ritually slaughtered. These rules are found in the Torah.

Research Task —

Research food in the two religions you are studying. Find out any rules. Which foods can/cannot be eaten?

Religious attitudes to the created world

Buddhism

Buddhists believe that all life, in whatever form, is sacred and special. Anything can develop and eventually achieve enlightenment. All life should be respected. Since everyone must live many, many times, it is important to protect the world for our own future, as well as our children's.

The DALAI LAMA has said:

- Destruction of nature and natural resources results from ignorance, greed and lack of respect for the Earth's living things. This lack of respect extends to future generations who will inherit a vastly degraded planet.

- The Earth is not only the common heritage of all humankind but also the ultimate source of life.

- Conservation is not merely a question of morality, but a question of our own survival.

Buddhism also teaches:

- Help, not harm other sentient beings (First Precept).

- Compassion for all life.

- There are karmic consequences to all of our actions.

Buddhists should respect the natural world. Rebirth means we will return to this world, and we must respect and not damage it. As one form of that respect, and reflecting the Precepts, most Buddhists are vegetarian. Animals are reborn beings on the same journey as humans and deserve respect. Buddhists will eat meat if it is offered to them (good will) and some Buddhists live in places such as Tibet, where the climate makes meat vital to a healthy diet. However, farming for meat feeds fewer people than farming for crops and can be cruel. For these reasons, being vegetarian shows COMPASSION.

Research Task —

Find out more about Buddhist food.

Christianity

Christians believe God created the world and gave mankind stewardship – the responsibility to look after the world. Christians in modern times especially have seen the need to work to heal the world and look after the environment.

Christianity teaches:

- God made the world and gave the duty of stewardship to humans (Genesis).

- The Earth is the Lord's and everything in it (Psalms).

- God gave the care of the animals to man and also permission to eat them (Genesis).

- Respect for life extends to the rest of creation (Pope John Paul II).

- More than ever – individually and collectively – people are responsible for the future of the planet (Pope John Paul II).

In Christianity, humans have a special role on Earth to look after the planet and animals. Humans are allowed to eat meat, but must not be cruel because animals are part of creation and deserve respect. This shows us that all life is sacred.

Since humans must face God on the DAY OF JUDGEMENT, everyone must carry out certain duties. If humans did not look after the world, or did nothing to stop its destruction, they should expect to be punished by God. This thought motivates many Christians to do environmental work.

Pope John Paul II was quite outspoken about ANIMAL RIGHTS. For example, he said the world should try to get rid of battery farms and animal experimentation because they are so unnatural, cruel and morally wrong. Both of these activities go against the duty of stewardship.

Research Task —

Find out more about St Francis of Assisi, patron saint of animals.

Hinduism

Traditionally, Hindu life was very simple and relied on the environment. This was linked with beliefs about the sanctity of life and non-violence to form a religion that is peaceful towards the environment. The cow is a sacred animal in Hinduism and protected in India.

Hinduism teaches:

- Respect for all life, including the created world.

- Ahimsa – non-violence.

- The cow is the symbol of purity, motherhood and non-violence.

- 'On a Brahmin … cow … elephant … dog … person of low caste, wise men look with equal eye.' (Bhagavad Gita)

- To focus on environmental values (as mentioned in the hymn Artharva Veda).

Most Hindus are vegetarians, reflecting their respect for life. Even the few who eat meat usually would not eat beef, because the cow is so sacred. All life is seen as interdependent, and that includes animal and plant life. All life depends on the environment, so everyone has a vested interest in protecting and looking after it. Additionally, Hindus believe our souls will all be reborn into more lifetimes on earth, so we have to look after it for our own future. God is seen as part of nature, so protection and worship are important as the Artharva Veda states.

Research Task –

Find out about attitudes to the cow in Hinduism or what the Artharva Veda says.

Islam

Islam sees the Creation in its entirety as the work of Allah. Humans are khalifa – stewards of the world. Looking after the world is important because it shows respect to Allah through his creation. Fulfilling the khalifa duty is a type of worship.

Islam teaches:

- 'The world is green and beautiful, and Allah has appointed you his stewards over it.' (Qur'an)

- 'The whole earth has been created as a place of worship.' (Qur'an)

- 'When Doomsday comes, if someone has a palm shoot in his hand, he should still plant it.' (Hadith)

- 'The Earth has been created for me as a mosque and a means of purification.' (Hadith)

- Green is the most important colour in Islam.

Humans live on Earth as trustees of Allah's creation. Trustees look after Allah's creation, rather than destroy it. Muslims believe they have a duty actively to look after the world. The QUR'AN says that those who do not follow their duty will be punished on Judgement Day by Allah. The whole creation reflects Allah and Allah knows everything that happens in it. Allah knows who damages and who looks after his creation. Muslims consider it a good idea to look after the world.

Islam says that Muslims are UMMAH – a brotherhood. This includes those in the past and future. Everyone has a duty to their family and fellow humans to make sure they pass on a world in which it is fit to live – not one damaged beyond repair because humans were so selfish as to think they could do what they wanted with it.

Research Task –

Find out the rules about halal food and halal butchery.

five

Judaism

Jewish sacred writings begin with God's creation of the world and go on to state that God gave man the duty of stewardship. Protection of animals is very important and there are many scriptures about this. Judaism has strict food rules about meat.

Judaism teaches:

- The Genesis creation story states that all is made by God and is good. Humans are given stewardship over the creation.

- The Bal tashchit (do not waste) precept in the TORAH can be interpreted as an instruction to conserve resources.

- 'The Earth and everything that is in it is the Lord's.' (Ketuvim)

- On the Sabbath day, all the family and the animals should not work. (Torah)

- 'A righteous man cares for the needs of his animal.' (Torah)

Jews have a duty to look after the world and should do this through treating it with respect. They should allow animals to rest, should not make it difficult for animals to eat and should care for them. Land is to be left fallow on a regular cycle. Increasingly, Jews are becoming more active in environmental work and are linking existing Jewish values to the issue. For example, tikkun olam (repairing the world) could be interpreted as tackling environmental problems; tzedek (justice) is being extended to mean justice for all of creation, including animals and the world itself.

Jewish food rules are very strict and begin with rules for looking after the animals and their slaughter. It is designed to make this as kind a process as possible.

Research Task –

Find out some recipes for Jewish food from the Sephardi tradition and the Ashkenazi tradition. Compare these two traditions.

Sikhism

Sikhs believe the natural environment is a gift from God and that we have to take care of it. The world only exists because of God, so God could stop the world existing. Sikhs believe the world is now in a 300-year cycle, known as the Cycle of Creation, which means there is a greater need to look after the world.

Sikhism teaches:

- The universe comes into being by God's will (Guru Nanak).

- 'In nature we see God, and in nature, we hear God speak'. (Adi Granth)

- Respect for all life.

- God created everything (Guru Nanak).

- The Sikh ideal is a simple life free from conspicuous waste.

Sikhs should look after the environment out of respect for life and as part of worship to God. Sikhs believe they must perform sewa (service) for others, and this can be understood to include the natural world. Of course, looking after the world means that it is safeguarded for future generations, so Sikhs are doing sewa for people in the future.

Sikh gurus have said that God is within everything, so damaging the world is like damaging God. Most Sikhs are vegetarians because of their respect for life. GURDWARAS have a LANGAR (food kitchen) that serves only vegetarian food. KHALSA vows forbid the eating of meat from an animal that has been ritually slaughtered. As part of the creation and a form of life, animals should be respected.

Research Task –

Find out about the origins of the langar and how it operates today.

Let's do some work

You have just read about the attitudes of the two religions you are studying to the created world. Don't forget the created world includes all of nature – plants and animals, as well as humans. The basic message of all religions is that all life is sacred, so respect it.

Don't forget to look back to pages 36–37 for the basic values from your two religions. These are valuable principles and beliefs to use in your answers.

Look forward to pages 98–99 because these pages have many ideas about how religions actually carry out that task of looking after the world.

Answer these questions for each of the two religions you are studying:

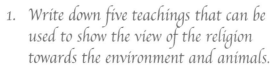

1. Write down five teachings that can be used to show the view of the religion towards the environment and animals.

2. For each teaching, explain what it means in relation to the environment.

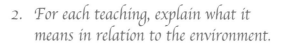

3. For each teaching, explain what it means in relation to animals.

4. Sum up in one paragraph the attitude of the religion to the environment.

5. Sum up in one paragraph the attitude of the religion to animals.

6. Describe and explain four ways in which a person in the religion could be a steward to the world.

7. Describe the work of an organisation in the religion that focuses on environmental issues (see pages 98–99).

Beliefs into action on the created world

There are lots of ways that religious people can look after the world. These pages give you examples of religious organisations, as well as some general ways that are open to people of any religion. You could do some extra research about any of the organisations from their website addresses.

Buddhism – organisation profile

Earth Sangha is a Buddhist group, based in Washington DC, USA. It is involved in projects of practical environmental action. It states that its work is 'informed with the principles of non-violence, tolerance, self-awareness and compassion'. These are all very important Buddhist values.

An example of its work is Native Forest Gardeners. This group is trying to re-establish the native plant populations around Washington DC, by growing them from seed and then replanting the saplings.

www.earthsangha.org

Christianity – organisation profile

The Christian Ecology Movement is a UK group that brings together Christians of all types to tackle environmental issues. It publishes a magazine and does a lot of education and campaigning work. It also gets involved in practical environmental action.

An example of its work is the LOAF food campaign, which encourages people to buy and eat food that fits only these categories – Locally produced; Organically grown; Animal friendly; Fairly traded. Operation Noah is their campaign to raise awareness of and push politicians to do something about climate change.

www.christian-ecology.org.uk

Pray

Hinduism – organisation profile

Friends of Vrindavan (FOV) is an organisation based in India and the UK. Its most important action is the Vrindavan Forest Revival Project. Vrindavan is a very poor area, with many environmental issues. This organisation helps both the environment and the people. The organisation is funded through money from the World Wildlife Fund and private donations from the UK.

Two of its projects are reforestation in Vrindavan and educating the people of Vrindavan, especially the children. FOV realises that educating people makes them understand the need for looking after the world, and encourages them to be involved.

www.fov.org.uk

Campaign

Be Vegetarian

Walk, don't drive

Judaism – organisation profile

The Coalition on the Environment and Jewish Life was set up in the USA in 1993. It tries to educate Jews in their religious responsibility to look after the world. It has reinterpreted many Jewish mitzvot and values to be about the created world. It supports and educates Jews on environmental matters, and creates opportunities for Jews to be involved in environmental action. It works with other religions to raise the profile of the environment as an issue.

Examples of its work include the Clean Car Campaign, which tries to educate people to use cars less and to switch to cleaner fuel types for their cars. It also helped to set up the Jewish Global Environmental Network, which is trying to solve some of Israel's environmental problems.

www.coejl.org

Grow a butterfly garden

Join an organisation

Sikhism – organisation profile

The Khalsa Environment Project was set up in 1999 in New Delhi. It tries to educate Sikhs about their responsibility to help the environment, believing that we have to educate young people to protect the future. A lot of their work is done in schools. It also educates through gurdwaras, emphasising the religious duty involved.

Its work includes tree planting in areas of deforestation and extending currently forested areas. It has also set up a better water-management project, which tries to educate about better use of a scarce yet vital resource.

www.khalsaenvironmentproject.org

Islam – organisation profile

The Islamic Foundation for Ecology and Environmental Science was set up in the mid-1980s. Its work focuses on research and education, especially in alternative technology. It is trying to find better ways to work, especially in poorer parts of the world where the environment is very fragile and people find it hard to survive.

Two of its projects are reforestation work in Mexico, and educating the people of Nigeria and Tanzania about Muslim conservation principles so that they can put them into action.

www.ifees.org

Pay for a tree to be planted

Eat organic

Now you know about how religious people look after the environment.

five

Exam Tips

What does a question on this topic look like?

This question is popular amongst candidates and comes up regularly on the exam. It can appear as two separate questions on the same paper – a question on the environment and a question on animals. It can also be combined with the topic of protest, so that you have to talk about organisations that fight for environmental issues and how they do that. However the topic appears, the question is always worth twenty marks. If there are two questions from this topic, they will stand against each other, so that you are only allowed to answer one of them. Answer both and you will only get marks for one (the one you did best on). If you do that, you will have wasted time and probably have failed to answer another question you should have completed.

Do you know everything about this topic?

There are many issues including experimentation, hunting, farming, zoos, genetic modification of animals, GM crops, consumption of natural resources, pollution, deforestation, global warming, destruction of natural habitats and animal and plant extinction. Can you explain the attitudes of both the religions you are studying to all those issues? It can appear difficult, as there are so many, but some tips are:

- Know a definition for each issue.

- Know some of the main problems that issue causes.

- Know the attitude of the religion to the environment or animals generally.

- Apply that attitude to that issue by way of the main problems.

There are some generalisations in answering this. Religions usually talk about:

- Life being sacred (sanctity of life).

- The world being God's creation.

- Humans having a role to look after the world and animals.

Ask yourself – does that issue conflict or agree with any of these general ideas? Use them as your starting point in explaining the attitude. Make sure you state the topic in your answer, so that it can't be read as a broad answer.

Explain the attitude of the two religions you have studied to deforestation.

This seems like a horrible question but it isn't really hard to answer.

The question would be worth six or eight marks for the two religions. That is three or four for one religion. Look at the ANSWER in the chart below – there is easily enough information there for full marks for one religion. Therefore it's not as difficult as it originally seemed. Try writing the answer for the other religion by following the FORMULA.

The FORMULA	The ANSWER
Firstly, explain what it means.	Deforestation is the deliberate cutting down of large areas of trees.
Secondly, what are the main issues?	This destroys the habitat of animals and can lead to extinction of species.
Thirdly, what is the religion's attitude to the environment?	Christianity believes God created the world, so it is sacred. God gave humans the responsibility to look after the world (stewardship), and doing that is an act of worship of God, as well as appreciation.
Finally, what does the attitude make them say about the issue?	By cutting down the forests, we destroy God's creation and endanger the lives of animals. This is not what stewardship means and is disrespectful to God.

five

Exam Tips

Candidates struggle most with questions that they have never had a chance to practice, as they aren't used to the way it is worded or they aren't familiar with the actual topic. Any work you do – even with a book full of notes in front of you – helps. It lets your brain see the question and think about exactly that kind of a query. When you see that type again in the exam, your brain doesn't panic and you can get on with answering it easily.

Try these questions and then try any other from the environment list:

Explain the attitudes of each of the two religions you have studied to …

a. genetic modification of crops

b. zoos

c. global warming

What if it's a question linked to protest?

There are three likely ways to be asked about this, and this is true for any topic on the course.

Firstly, you could be asked *why* they protest. That is easy – *because they don't agree with it*. But what if the question is worth four marks – that answer would receive one mark maximum. Extend your answer by showing *why they don't agree with it*. Which of the principles of the religion does it go against? For example, genetic modification goes against the idea that God created things exactly as he wanted them.

You could also be asked *how* they protest. Again it is easy – list the ways anybody else protests. For example, campaigning, marching, petitioning and so on. Mention the non-violent ways, as that is how most religious people protest.

Finally, you could be asked to describe the work of a religious organisation that protests. Describe their work on this; don't give lots of information about their history. Name the group; say what they do and how effective it has been. There are things they all do –such as run campaigns to raise awareness or get the Government to change the law or get people to behave differently. Even if you know almost nothing besides the name of an organisation, writing about campaigning will get you one or more marks.

Appendix 1

Revision checklist

This section provides an outline of each topic in the specification, and shows where to find it in the book. Use the guide as a checklist of what you know, and what you have still got to get to grips with.

It also works as a last-minute summary of your knowledge before the exam. When you have

finished all your revision, you should be able to recognise each word. Each phrase should trigger a whole range of ideas in your head – linked people, examples and explanations. Read through the revision chart twice, thinking of each of your religions in turn, to revise both faiths properly.

UNIT	WORDS TO LEARN	TOPICS WITHIN UNIT – DO YOU KNOW…?
Public and private worship (Unit 1)	*Learn the correct word for each of these:* Prayer/meditation Aids to worship Sacred text Religious leader Symbols of faith Religious service	• How they pray/meditate • Why they pray/meditate • How they use aids to worship • Why these are important • What the symbols represent • Why sacred texts are important • How sacred texts are used in an act of worship • How they pray and give thanks in their place of worship • How they worship at home • Why they might prefer to worship at home or in a place of worship • The role of the religious leader • Why the religious leader is important
Places of worship (Unit 1)	*Learn the correct word for each of these:* Place of worship Furnishings within a place of worship	• How to recognise a place of worship from the outside • What items of furniture you'd find in a place of worship • What those items are used for or represent • What a home shrine might look like
Human sexuality and sexual relationships (Unit 4)	Chastity Celibacy Heterosexuality Homosexuality Age of consent Sex before marriage Adultery	• Why we have or don't have sexual relationships • Religious attitude to sex • Religious attitude to sex before marriage • Why we have an age of consent • Why some people disagree with homosexuality • Religious attitude to homosexuality • Why people generally think adultery to be wrong • Religious attitude to adultery

UNIT	WORDS TO LEARN	TOPICS WITHIN UNIT – DO YOU KNOW…?
Married and family life (Unit 4)	Covenant/contract Vows/promises Marriage Responsibility Roles Birth/initiation ceremonies	• Why people marry • What promises people make when marrying • What the marriage ceremony is like, including its symbolism • The roles of men and women in marriage as father and mother, husband and wife • What birth/initiation ceremonies are like • How religious people should bring up their children
Issues in human relationships (Unit 4)	Contraception Artificial forms of contraception Abortion Sanctity of life Quality of life Divorce Remarriage	• Which forms of contraception religious people use • Religious attitude to the use of contraception • Why women have abortions • The law about abortion • Religious attitude to abortion • Examples of when religious believers generally would accept an abortion is necessary • Why couples divorce • Religious attitude to divorce • Religious attitude to remarriage • The work of a protest group about abortion
Prejudice and discrimination (Unit 3)	Prejudice Discrimination Equality Justice Community Sexism Racism Religious prejudice Homophobia Ageism	• Why people are prejudiced • How people show their prejudice • Religious attitude to prejudice generally • Religious attitude to all specific types of prejudice – racism, sexism, homophobia, ageism, religious prejudice • How religions fight against prejudice and discrimination • How religions help the victims of prejudice and discrimination • The work of a protest group about prejudice and discrimination
Animals and the environment (Unit 5)	Responsibility Stewardship Creation Sanctity of life Community Environment Vegetarianism Animal experimentation Factory farming Zoos	• The problem with trying to help humans and protect the environment • How people damage the environment • How people help the environment • Religious attitude to the natural world • Religious attitude to animal rights • Religious attitude to eating meat, and food in general • Religious attitude to any specific topic from the list on the left, from 'Animal experimentation' onwards

UNIT	WORDS TO LEARN	TOPICS WITHIN UNIT – DO YOU KNOW…?
Unit 5 continued …	Hunting Genetic modification of animals Genetic modification of crops Consumption of natural resources Pollution Deforestation Global warming Destruction of natural habitats	• The work of a protest group about the environment • The work of a protest group about animal rights • The work of an environmental organisation
Protest, pressure groups and minority rights (Unit 2)	Protest Non-violent protest Conscientious objection Pressure groups Minority rights Equality Sanctity of life Community Responsibility	• Why people protest in general terms • Why people protest about specific issues • How people protest in general terms • How people protest about specific issues • Non-violent means of protest • The work of pressure groups • How we should treat minority groups in society • Links between this topic and all the others

Appendix II

Sample Paper

What a question paper looks like

You will be given a question paper and an answer booklet in the examination.

Although it might not seem worth reading the front cover of the paper because they all seem to be the same, it is worth looking at this page of the exam. It is easy in a stressful time to mix up what you are meant to do. Probably your teacher will have told you a million times what you have to do, but you can still forget. It is a good idea just to check through the cover – if nothing else, it is a calming exercise and helps if you are nervous. It also reassures you that you do know exactly what you are doing.

The cover will remind you:

- How long the exam lasts so you can plan and use your time well. Reassess how long you have left after answering each full section, as you might have gained or lost time. Don't spend too much time on one question, but don't rush yourself either.

- Which questions you must answer – Question A.

- Which questions you get a choice of – **either** B2 **or** B3, **either** B4 **or** B5, and **either** B6 **or** B7. If you answer them all, you'll be given marks for the best one from each pair, but you will have wasted a lot of time. Some people find they have lots of time left over when they have finished, so they answer extra questions to pass the time! Examiners don't recommend this. If you do, the Examiner will mark all of them, and take the highest mark to add to your overall mark.

- That you must write about the same two religions throughout the paper. It is a good idea to answer every question twice, once for each religion. Your answer will be much clearer and therefore easier to mark.

- That you should write the names of the two religions you studied on the front of your answer booklet. Don't worry if you don't – no marks are lost. It is just a reminder to you and a help to the examiner.

- To use blue or black ink/pen. This makes your paper easier to read and mark.

- That you should do any notes or practice work either on your answer booklet or on extra paper. Sometimes, people write correct things that they then don't put into their real answer. If you hand in all your practice work and notes, the examiner can credit you for anything you missed. They are obliged to read it all.

So much for the cover, what about the inside?

Section A will be a page of pictures – one for each religion – and a page with some questions on it. You have to answer this. The pictures are meant to stimulate your brain and start you thinking. In other words, they are meant to help you by triggering the relevant ideas.

Section B is in three parts, each offering a choice of one of two questions. They are usually from connected areas of the specification. Answer one of each two.

SECTION A

Answer all parts of this question

You must answer all the questions. Make sure you do it for both religions

A1 Worship: *The topic*

Look at the pictures below:

They are meant to get your brain working

Buddhist place of worship

Christian place of worship

Hindu place of worship

Muslim place of worship

Jewish place of worship

Sikh place of worship

(a) Name the place of worship in each of the religions you are studying. (2 marks)

(b) For each of the two religions you are studying, describe an act of worship that is carried out in the place of worship. (6 marks)

Split your answer into two distinct sections, one for each religion

(c) Why might some people prefer to worship at home? (3 marks)

(d) Explain why religious people believe it is important to pray or meditate. (4 marks)

Don't just list reasons, explain them

(e) 'It is important to read sacred texts regularly if you are religious.' Do you agree with this statement? Give reasons and explain your answer, showing you have thought about more than one point of view. (5 marks)

Remember DREARE

SECTION B

Answer **either** Question B2 **or** Question B3
Each question carries 20 marks

Don't do both or you will waste time

EITHER

B2 Prejudice and Discrimination

Section B questions may have a stimulus such as a news headline, picture or chart

---

**RACE HATE CRIMES AT
ALL-TIME HIGH**

(a) What is the difference between *prejudice* and *discrimination?* (2 marks)

Split your answer into two distinct sections, one for each religion

(b) Explain the attitude of the two religions you have studied to the issue of racial prejudice. (8 marks)

Make your answer specific

(c) Explain the ways in which a religious believer could try to help those who suffer from prejudice and discrimination. (5 marks)

Don't just list, explain

(d) 'A woman's true place is in the home.' Do you agree with this statement? Give reasons and explain your answer, showing you have thought about more than one point of view. Refer to religious arguments in your answer. (5 marks)

If you don't give at least one religious idea, you can't get more than 3 marks.

Remember DREARE – two sides and two or more reasons for each, all explained

OR

B3 Abortion and Protest

ANGRY PROTESTS OUTSIDE
ABORTION CLINIC – NURSE HURT
TRYING TO ENTER

(a)   State *two* reasons why a woman might want to have an abortion. (2 marks)

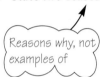

Reasons why, not examples of

(b)   Explain the attitude of the two religions you have studied to the issue of abortion. (8 marks)

(c)   Explain the ways in which a religious believer could protest in this situation. (5 marks)

Religious believers should be non-violent so try to keep to those ways

(d)   'Abortion should be available on demand.' Do you agree with this statement? Give reasons and explain your answer, showing you have thought about more than one point of view. Refer to religious arguments in your answer. (5 marks)

Look at how the marks mirror those for the alternative question

SECTION B

Answer **either** Question B4 **or** Question B5
Each question carries 20 marks

EITHER

B4 The Environment

(a) What do we mean by the word *stewardship*? (1 mark)

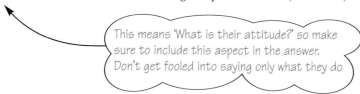

No stimulus here as there doesn't need to be

(b) Explain how humans damage the environment. (4 marks)

(c) Explain how religious believers in each of the two religions you have studied should treat the world. Refer to beliefs and teachings in your answer. (10 marks)

This means 'What is their attitude?' so make sure to include this aspect in the answer. Don't get fooled into saying only what they do

(d) 'If everyone helped a bit, there'd be no environmental problems.' Do you agree with this statement? Give reasons and explain your answer, showing you have thought about more than one point of view. Refer to religious arguments in your answer. (5 marks)

OR

B5 Animal Rights

(a) What do we mean by *animal rights*? (1 mark)

As it is only worth one mark, don't write lots. One sentence should be enough

(b) Explain why some people disagree with live experimentation. (4 marks)

Make your answer specific to animals

Only answer from the disagree viewpoint or you'll waste time

(c) Explain how religious believers in each of the two religions you have studied are expected to treat animals. Refer to beliefs and teachings in your answer. (10 marks)

(d) 'Eating meat just encourages animal cruelty.'
Do you agree with this statement? Give reasons and explain your answer, showing you have thought about more than one point of view. Refer to religious arguments in your answer.
(5 marks)

You can't get more than three marks, no matter how good your answer is, if you don't include some religious ideas in your answer

SECTION B

Answer **either** Question B6 **or** Question B7
Each question carries 20 marks

Don't do both, choose the one you are best at

EITHER

B6 Sex, Marriage and Divorce

(a) Why do people choose to marry? (3 marks)

Just give three simple reasons

(b) Describe a marriage ceremony in each of the two religions you have studied. (8 marks)

(c) Explain why some religious people disagree with divorce. (4 marks)

Make sure your answer includes religious reasons or you won't get full marks

(d) 'Contraception encourages people to cheat on their husband or wife.' Do you agree with this statement? Give reasons and explain your answer, showing you have thought about more than one point of view. Refer to religious arguments in your answer. (5 marks)

OR

B7 Children and Birth/Initiation Ceremonies

When it asks you for answers from two religions, the mark will usually be split equally between the two religions.

(a) Why do people choose to have children? (3 marks)

(b) Describe a birth or initiation ceremony in each of the two religions you have studied. (8 marks)

(c) Explain how a religious couple might bring up their children. (4 marks)

(d) 'It is important to have children within marriage.' Do you agree? Give reasons and explain your answer, showing you have thought about more than one point of view. Refer to religious arguments in your answer. (5 marks)

Glossary

ABORTION – the deliberate expulsion of a foetus from the womb with the intent to destroy it

ABORTION RIGHTS – an organisation that fights for women's rights to access to abortion

ADULTERY – having an affair

AGEISM – discrimination against someone because of age

AGE OF CONSENT – the age at which it is legal to have sex

AIDS TO WORSHIP – items used as a focus in worship

ALTAR – the focal point of a church

ANIMAL RIGHTS – the belief that animals have rights because they are sentient beings, so should receive respect and protection

ANNULMENT – cancellation of marriage

ARK OF THE COVENANT – the focal point of a synagogue

AUM – the sacred symbol and sound of Hinduism

BHIKKHU – a Buddhist monk (Theravada)

BIBLE – sacred writing of Christianity

BIRTH CEREMONIES – rituals to mark the birth of a child, for example, baptism (Christianity), Tahneek (Islam)

BRAHMIN PRIEST – a Hindu religious leader

BUDDHA – the founder of Buddhism

CELIBACY – a conscious decision to abstain from sexual relationships

CHASTITY – purity; refraining from sex before marriage

CHURCH – Christian place of worship

COMMUNION – Christian act of worship, remembering the sacrifice of Jesus for humanity

COMMUNITY – group of people

COMPASSION – loving kindness

CONSCIENTIOUS OBJECTION – refusal to do something on the grounds of it being against one's beliefs

CONTRACEPTION – method of prevention of pregnancy or sexually transmitted diseases

COVENANT – agreement

CREATION – belief that the world was deliberately made by God from nothing

CROSS – symbol of Christianity to remember that Jesus rose from the dead and ascended to heaven

CRUCIFIX – symbol of Christianity to remember the sacrifice of Jesus for humanity

DALAI LAMA – religious leader of Tibetan Buddhist movement

DHARMACHAKRA – symbol of Buddhism

DISCRIMINATION – actions based on prejudice, often negative

DIVORCE – legal cancellation of marriage bond

DIWAN – Sikh act of worship

ENVIRONMENTAL ISSUES – problems to do with the environment, for example, pollution, deforestation etc.

EQUALITY – concept of everyone having the same value, so deserving the same rights and respect

FARE – Football Against Racism in Europe, an organisation that unites the many football-based anti-racist groups around Europe

FAWCETT SOCIETY – society in the UK dedicated to gaining equality in all areas for women

FIVE Ks – five symbols of Sikhism that all Sikhs wear/carry

FIVE PRECEPTS – five guidelines for living that all Buddhists follow

GRANTHI – person who reads from the Guru Granth Sahib in Sikh worship

GURDWARA – Sikh place of worship

GURU GRANTH SAHIB – Sikh sacred writing

HADITH – book of the deeds and sayings of Prophet Muhammad ﷺ

HETEROSEXUALITY – physical attraction to a person of the opposite sex

HOMOPHOBIA – prejudice against homosexuality

HOMOSEXUALITY – physical attraction to a person of the same sex

IMAM – Muslim religious leader

INITIATION CEREMONIES – ceremonies held to welcome someone into a religion officially

JUDGEMENT DAY – In Christianity, Islam and Judaism, the day at the end of time when God judges each person to decide whether they should go to heaven or hell

JUSTICE – fairness

KA'BAH – the direction Muslims must face when praying, representing the Ka'bah shrine in Mecca where Muhammad prayed

KETUBAH – Jewish marriage contract

KHALSA – term for initiated Sikhs who follow the religion closely

KHANDA – symbol of Sikhism

LANGAR – Sikh communal food kitchen/meal, which originated in Kartarpur with Guru Nanak

MALA – Buddhist/Hindu/Sikh prayer beads

MANDIR – Hindu place of worship

MARRIAGE – legal binding of two people as a couple; believed to be blessed by God in many religions

MEDITATION – focusing or concentrating to learn religious truths

MENORAH – seven-branched candlestick; symbol of Judaism

MINORITY RIGHTS – the idea that small groups deserve rights, justice and protection

MONASTICISM – the concept of devoting life to God/religion and not entering into close/sexual relationships with others

MOOL MANTRA – basic statement of Sikh belief about God

MOSQUE – Muslim place of worship

MUHAMMAD ﷺ – Prophet and founder of Islamic faith

NER TAMID – everlasting light, representing God

NIKKAH – Muslim marriage contract

NON-VIOLENT PROTEST – protest that uses peaceful means

OFFERINGS – gifts made to God/Buddha at the place of worship, usually food, flowers, incense or money

PALKI AND TAKHT – the throne and canopy that protect/elevate the Guru Granth Sahib in a gurdwara

POPE – religious leader of the Roman Catholic faith

PRAYER – quiet thoughts directed to God/deity

PREJUDICE – attitude, usually negative, to someone without knowing them

PRESSURE GROUP – group/organisation set up to force politicians/companies to change their practice, usually because of ethical concerns

PROTEST – making feelings against something known

PUJA – Hindu act of worship

QIBLAH WALL – focal part of mosque, which shows direction for prayer

QUR'AN – Muslim sacred writings

RABBI – Jewish religious leader

RACISM – prejudice and discrimination against someone because of the colour of their skin

REINCARNATION – the belief that our soul/self will be born and reborn many times

REMARRIAGE – marriage after divorce

RESPONSIBLE PARENTHOOD – the idea that a couple should have only as many children as they can properly look after

SACRAMENT – ritual act, which brings blessing from God; outward sign of inward grace

SALAH – Islamic duty of prayer

SANCTITY OF LIFE – the idea that all life is sacred/special

SANGHA – community of Buddhist monks

SEXISM – prejudice and discrimination against someone because of their gender

SHRINE – the focus for worship, usually containing religious objects

STEWARDSHIP – the idea that we have a duty given by God to look after the created world

SYNAGOGUE – Jewish place of worship

TASBI – Muslim prayer beads

TEMPLE – Buddhist place of worship

TEN COMMANDMENTS – ten basic rules for living found in the Torah/Old Testament

TIPITAKA – Buddhist sacred writings

TORAH SCROLL – Jewish sacred writings

UMMA – the Muslim idea of brotherhood between all Muslim believers

VEGETARIANISM – a diet that does not include meat

VICAR – a Christian religious leader (Church of England)

VOWS – Christian marriage promises

WORSHIP – an act of devotion made to God

Index